The Human Spark - Beyond AI

CHRISTIAN KROMME

THE CHOIR PRESS

First published in the United Kingdom in 2026 by
The Choir Press

Paperback ISBN 978-1-78963-594-2
Hardback ISBN 978-1-78963-596-6

Contents

Preface - Welcome to The Human Spark - Beyond AI

Today, humanity stands at a crossroads. For the first time in human history, we have technology that exceeds our cognitive capabilities that have been our defining advantage through evolution. This creates an existential question: if machines can think better than us, what makes us uniquely valuable as human beings? This question is not just philosophical - it is intensely practical.

As AI and automation accelerates, millions of jobs based on routine cognitive tasks will disappear. Many of us will be forced to confront difficult questions about our identity, purpose, and value in a world where machines do much of the thinking. But within this challenge lies an unprecedented opportunity. As machines take over routine cognitive tasks, we can rediscover and develop our uniquely human qualities - our creativity, intuition, empathy, and ability to find and create meaning.

In my previous book, "Humanification - Go Digital, Stay Human," I explored how we could thrive in a world of rapidly advancing technology. As the pace of technological change accelerates, it's becoming increasingly clear that we're on the cusp of a new era that will demand even more from us.

We will delve deeper into what it means to be human in the context of the Fourth Industrial Revolution and answer the most important questions of our age; are humans going to compete with machines, or will we be forced to develop in another direction? How will technology change us? What kind of mindset and skills will we need to stay relevant?

Hopi elder Dan Evehema said: "In the future, there will be two kinds of human beings - those who are aligned with the spirit and those who are aligned with technology." That resonates because I have struggled to balance my reliance on technology with my desire to stay connected to my humanity and my spirituality.

I see the same struggles in others, even if they don't recognise it themselves. In the future, there may be two streams of humanity. One enlightened enough to maintain their true spirit, understand their true essence and who can connect with nature and the universe. The other who will become mechanical beings who have lost touch with themselves and become slaves to technology.

I value being in tune with my inner self and connecting with the world. I want to strive to become a spiritual being instead of a mechanical one. If this resonates with you, then allow this book to guide you.

The Fourth Industrial Revolution promises to bring about transformative changes to our society, economy, and our daily lives. They are going to bring many new challenges and opportunities, so to thrive, you need to be prepared.

We will explore what's coming and how you can balance technology and spirituality. This is your chance to glimpse into the future of technology while doing some self-exploration and understand what it's all going to mean for your life, career and family. We will look at new industries, jobs, technology, our own personal development and the skills and mindsets necessary for success.

The goal is not to reject technology, but to balance utilising it while keeping a connection with our true human spirit. We can consciously decide to become the kind of humans we want to be, and explore humanity in the context of our rapidly changing world.

A Crossroads for Human Kind

Intelligence has been our defining advantage. It has allowed us to survive, thrive, and dominate our environment. Our capacity to think, reason, and solve complex problems has set us apart from all other species. But today, machines are beginning to out think us. As AI advances at an exponential pace, we face a profound question: What makes us uniquely human when machines can process information faster, make better decisions, and even show creativity?

The convergence of physical, digital, and biological technologies are going to fundamentally alter how we live, work, and relate to one another. Previous industrial revolutions primarily changed what we could do, this one challenges who we are.

A Personal Journey

My journey toward understanding the future of mankind began in a hospital room. In 2012, my three-month-old daughter was diagnosed with a rare genetic disorder. The doctors told us she had no chance of survival.

That forced me to question everything I thought I knew about technology, medicine, and human potential. Rather than accepting conventional wisdom, I began researching holistic approaches to healing. What I discovered changed not only my daughter's life, but my entire perspective on human evolution and technology. I found that by looking at problems holistically, rather than through the narrow lens of specialisation, entirely new solutions became possible.

My daughter not only survived but thrived, defying all medical predictions. This experience taught me a profound lesson: the greatest breakthroughs often come NOT from increasing specialisation, but from seeing the bigger picture and the interconnections that narrow focused specialisation can miss. The same principle applies to our relationship with technology and AI.

It's Not Man Vs Machine

We don't need to compete with machines at their own game. Instead, we can transcend the old paradigm of human-machine competition and move toward a human-machine collaboration - where technology amplifies our humanity, rather than replaces it. We will need to shift our focus from developing hard skills that machines will increasingly master, to cultivating our softer, more human skills. It means moving from an ego-based model of competition to an eco-based model of collaboration and rediscovering our connection to nature, each other, and our own deeper purpose.

Until now, much industrialisation and progress has been at the expense of mother nature and human nature. A shift in thinking could bring us back onto the same side.

The Path Forward

Through research, case studies, and practical exercises, we will explore:

- The seven evolutionary waves that have brought us to where we are today
- The key shifts in consciousness needed to thrive in the age of AI
- The skills that will become increasingly more valuable
- Why they are so crucial in fluid future organisations
- Ways to find and align with your deeper purpose
- Practical steps for evolving from human 3.0 to human 4.0

The journey from Human 3.0 to Human 4.0 is about adapting to new technology and rediscovering our essential humanity simultaneously.

Industry 4.0 integrates advanced technologies including A.I., robotics, 3D printing, Augmented Reality, the Internet of Things (IoT), blockchain and automation. With the pace of technological change happening so rapidly, it's increasingly difficult for individuals and businesses to keep up and make strategic decisions.

As automation and artificial intelligence become more prevalent many jobs are going to become redundant, though new roles needing different skills are going to be created. The huge changes in the labour market are going to be deeply challenging to navigate. Advancing technology brings income inequality, privacy, and other concerns that we will discuss.

Those who are aware of the challenges will be able to take steps to address them. Those who aren't will be left behind.

Part I

Chapter 1

Navigating The Fourth Industrial Revolution

Our world is going digital at warp speed and many relatively new technologies are already impacting our world more than most people realise. As advances move from the edges into the mainstream, they are triggering seismic shifts in business and the way we work and our personal lives will transform in ways we haven't even considered.

Technology is moving closer to our physical selves too. It is literally getting under our skin. In Sweden, more than 3,000 people have implanted chips into their hands. They can book a train ticket just using their chip, taking wearable technology further than most people thought would be acceptable only a decade ago. We are biohacking our way to longer lives and hacking happiness.

Many futurists and scientists believe that by 2030, people will be living for 150 years or more. Biohacking will allow us to access parts of ourselves that monks had to meditate for decades to reach. Add to that the exponential advances in our understanding of the connection between our minds and bodies, improved treatments for disease, and our ability to read and alter our DNA, our time on this planet will be transformed.

But all that progress won't deliver a better world unless we push ourselves to evolve our thinking and behaviours to keep up. If we fail to develop our thinking as quickly as the technology revolution is happening, we risk becoming empty vessels with little to contribute.

Many jobs will be automated by intelligent technology, probably within the next decade. We will all be challenged to answer serious questions about our purpose and usefulness. As our technology makes us progressively more redundant, we are going to be forced to answer some challenging questions including;

- Who are we, and why are we here?
- What does it mean to be Human?
- How do I lead my life, and what does practical work look like?

We will explore how you can stay ahead of the curve, whether you're an individual looking to up-skill or a business looking to remain relevant and competitive.

Chapter 2

The Big Transition

We humans are well adapted to gradual, linear change, but our world is changing in a very non-linear way. Sudden big shifts are replacing gradual change, and many people won't see what's coming until it's too late.

Everything we discuss is part of, and connected to, a larger whole, though things are far less complicated than they first appear. By understanding the connected elements you can navigate through the apparent complexity and develop a future-proof mindset to help you stay relevant and fulfilled.

Your future-proof mindset starts by building a more holistic perspective of the world around you, organisations, technology, and yourself.

There are four essential quadrants to know about that give you a holistic worldview to navigate your future with.

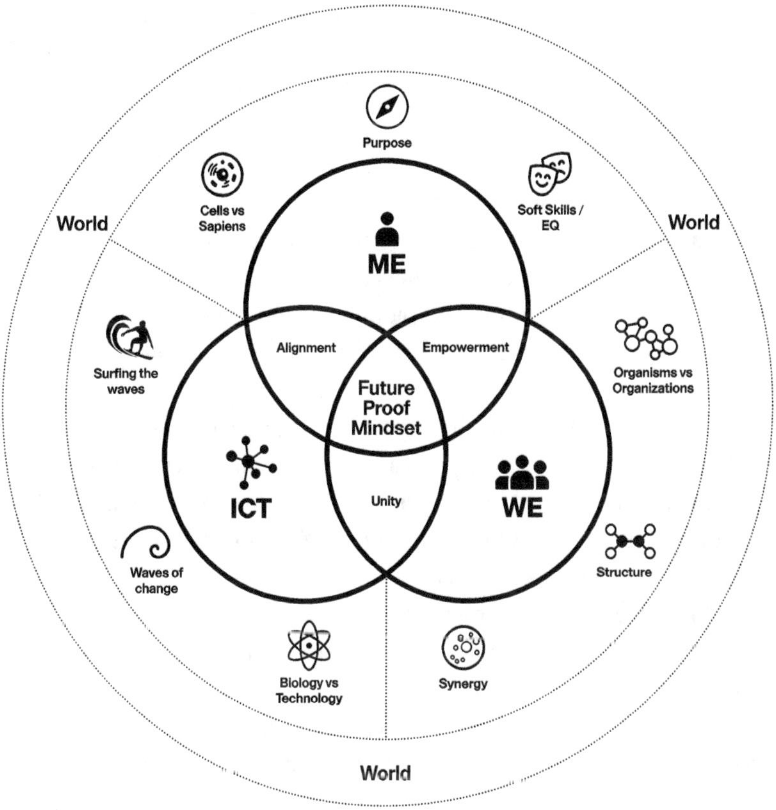

Your Future Proof Mindset

The outer circle explores the WORLD around us. How did it come into being, and what are the driving forces behind the scenes? When you understand those forces, you can see the connection between societal, technological, organisational, and your own personal developments. Everything starts to make sense. This foundation gives you the lens through which you can view the inner circle, namely the ME, the individual (you, me) and how we fit in.

Next, we look at the critical purpose in our lives and how it relates to long-term happiness. We explore the importance of soft human skills and emotional intelligence to examine the WE; that's the collective, our culture, and organisations.

There are remarkable parallels and patterns common to both biological organisms and technological organisations. They reveal the magic of what nature teaches us, and how to apply those patterns to predict what's coming next.

We can learn a great deal from the organising forces and structures of nature. We'll look at swarm organisations, synergetic organisational cultures and how they could change the way we work.

We will zoom in on the parallels between biology and technology and use them to predict future disruptive waves of technology. You can anticipate those disruptions when you understand how technology itself evolves.

Finally, we will explore how you can move from anticipating to participating. Like a surfer, you can predict when a wave is coming, see when it's rising, and know the optimum time to start surfing. You can connect the dots by zooming out to gain a different perspective. You will see how technology can

- Empower people to focus on their purpose or passion
- Unite groups of people in larger organisations
- How organisations can behave like a super-organism.

Technology has the power to create unity and alignment in organisations when we know how to focus on the right things.

It's All About Perception

All the most valuable training I've had in recent years has been training that has changed my perception of things. Changing perspective creates new awareness and consciousness that expands your whole world view. When awareness and consciousness shifts, you can change almost effortlessly. When you see things differently, you act differently.

Take a look at this picture.

What do you see, a rabbit, or a duck?

You brain will see either one or the other. If you have seen pictures of rabbits recently, you might find it difficult to see the picture of the duck - and vice versa. The neural networks in your brain process the image in a binary way. If they are trained to see rabbits, then you'll see the rabbit first. And so it is for the choices you make every day. How your neural networks are structured determine how you see the world.

You can train your brain to see things differently by offering it different patterns. You only need a tiny perspective shift to switch from the rabbit to duck, or to switch from seeing threats, to seeing opportunities.

"Sometimes all it takes is a tiny shift of perspective to see something familiar in a new light."

Dan Brown

Chapter 3

Meet Human 3.0 - Product of the 3rd Industrial Revolution

For generations, our worldview has been shaped by past industrial revolutions. We have been defined by how well we could follow rules, climb the ladder, and master a specific skillset. We have all been brought up to believe that our intelligence was measured by our ability to be logical and efficient. Progress was built on predictability, control, and hierarchy. But as we stand on the brink of the Fourth Industrial Revolution, this mindset is being challenged.

Today you can control your entire home using your voice. Cars have the capability to drive themselves. You can connect with someone on the other side of the world with a click. All this is thanks to the 3rd Industrial Revolution.

The 1st Industrial Revolution saw the introduction of steam power and the mechanisation of the textile industry. The 2nd Industrial Revolution brought mass production, assembly lines, and the rise of the car industry. The 3rd Industrial Revolution brought us the digital technology that has transformed our world.

The Digital Revolution brought us Personal Computers and the Internet that revolutionised how we communicate and access information. We pay our bills, research, travel, book flights, interact with government, shop, bank, pay to park and access health services online. Those who aren't online are being left further and further behind.

Cloud computing and big data analytics have enabled the creation of smart machines and systems that collect and analyse vast amounts of data, helping to make more informed and automated decisions.

In the 1980s, Personal Computers appeared and the internet began to take shape. In the 90's, the World Wide Web was developed and e-commerce emerged as a new way of doing business. The 2000s saw the rise of social media. More recently our internet enabled mobile devices have changed the way we interact with each other and e-commerce, social media, and mobile apps have transformed our lives.

New jobs were created; data scientists, cybersecurity experts, and software developers, all requiring highly specialised skills that brought in remote working and the gig economy.

New skills and mindsets were needed to succeed; data analysis, coding, and digital literacy became essential. Soft skills like adaptability and collaboration became more highly valued. The Digital Revolution turned the traditional employer-employee relationship on its head. The COVID lockdowns further entrenched the changes.

An essential quality in such a rapidly evolving digital landscape is a growth mindset focused on continuous learning and improvement. We have moved further already, to a time when a mindset of innovation, disruption, and risk-taking is increasingly valued. That's a very different to the mindset of the blind compliance that dominated just a decade ago.

As the Digital Revolution continues to mature, a level playing field has emerged where startups and small businesses can compete with larger organisations on equal terms. You no longer have to build a bespoke payment platform yourself, to code training systems, or write HTML to build a website or market to a global audience. Until recently these were huge barriers to do business in a global market. Today, they are available to a sole trader for a minimal monthly cost. This cheap access to technology is the foundation for the 4th Industrial Revolution. As we move further into the digital age, expect even more changes to how we live, work, and do business.

More Access, Yet More Inequality

Not everyone has benefited from the Digital Revolution. As new industries and jobs emerged, many workers have been left behind and Income inequality is at record levels. As we move into the 4th Industrial Revolution, I believe that we must create a more equitable and inclusive society. We need to invest in education and training so more people have the skills to succeed. People who adapt and embrace it will thrive, those who can't will be left even further behind.

The 3rd Industrial Revolution - Skills and Jobs

The Digital Revolution was built on the foundation of hard skills and repetitive tasks that came before it, mainly in the manufacturing and service sectors. There were high numbers of machine operators working with large, complex machines to work metal and keep production going when things went wrong, jobs that played a crucial role in the economy. Workers with specific hard skills were in high demand and had good earning power, but automation and digital technology have made such jobs increasingly rare.

Only a few years ago, when businesses were transitioning to digital records, huge numbers of people entered large amounts of data into spreadsheets and databases. Workers needed a strong understanding of data entry software to work quickly and accurately. But things have changed. Online forms, speech to text functionality and software that reads pdf's and human handwriting has massively reduced the number of office based repetitive jobs.

Retail used to depend on cashiers to process sales transactions, handle cash and cards and provide customer service. Many of these roles have been automated and some stores have no people at check outs at all.

There were significant benefits of such jobs. People had a level of stability and reasonable pay, trading but had a lack of flexibility and limited opportunities for growth or advancement. It was a trade-off that many were happy with.

As automation and digital technology advances, we will see a more accelerated shift toward jobs needing soft skills, problem-solving abilities, and creative thinking and we will need to need to adapt if we want to stay relevant.

3rd Industrial Revolution - Mindset Limitations

During the 3rd Industrial Revolution, efficiency, hard work, and a willingness to do repetitive tasks served us well. But they aren't adequate for the challenges of the future, as many people are finding out. Almost gone are the days where people were typically focused on doing their jobs well, meeting targets and doing long hours of repetitive work. Those employed by large organisations were expected to conform to rules and expectations set by the company, but that mindset hinders us.

The premium on efficiency and repetition is being replaced with a premium on creativity and innovation. As future challenges become more complex and nuanced, people who can think critically, collaborate, and devise creative solutions to problems will be in high demand.

Conformity that stifles creativity will be out; innovation that sparks new ideas will be in.

Chapter 4

Bottom Up Thinking - How It Holds Us Back

Many of today's dominant institutions and organisations emerged during the 3rd Industrial Revolution, and even though much has changed for the better because of it, conventional thinking is preventing people and organisations from evolving as fast as the environment they now find themselves in.

Society has been dominated by left brain rational and logical thinking for decades. The academic subjects of mathematics, chemistry, and physics use our left brain hemisphere. Our educational systems and economics have focused on the development and exploitation of this style of thinking. It was an asset in the mechanical age when we were educating people for large system based enterprises. Today, we still live in a society driven and dominated by scientific insights that brought us to where we are now, but that approach won't take us to the next phase. Technology is moving too fast, we don't have time.

The relatively stable industrialised world that we are leaving behind changed relatively slowly. We managed complexity by dividing a complex problem into smaller problems, which were divided again into ever smaller problems. This approach was applied in almost all traditional hierarchical organisations across government, military, science, medicine, and almost all large commercial organisations. But tomorrow's world is too complex to manage using this old compartmentalised thinking.

The late Bruce Lee said "It's like a finger pointing to the moon. Don't concentrate on the finger or you will miss all that heavenly glory." When we view sub-issues as separate entities, we end up concentrating on the finger, missing the larger heavens and finding more finger problems. By the time we have solved them, the moon is no longer visible. The time or budget to fix the big problem we aimed to solve has run out.

Medical science is a good example of our current way of managing complexity. We study the workings of the body by dividing it into anatomically smaller pieces; organs, tissues, cells, proteins, and molecules. We know what each minor part does, but it's easily missed that each minor part is an integral part of a larger whole. Thanks to scientists, MRI, ultrasound, powerful microscopes and communication technology, we know what diseases do to our organs and tissues. Yet in many cases, we have no idea what the underlying causes of many diseases are. As a result, we practice symptom suppression on a massive scale.

This happens in politics and business as well. Too many specialists concentrate on the finger and don't see the moon at all.

Our hierarchically organised systems are groaning and cracking everywhere. Our old style thinking is causing many of the global crises unfolding before our eyes; problems in politics, food, energy, health, finance, and resource availability are symbolising the end of our old-thinking era.

To break free and progress from old patterns we need to combine our current scientific way of thinking with a more holistic one. Holistic thinking is a more natural way of thinking that we have been educated out of. It considers all parts and looks at the broader context as one integral whole, more like a living ecosystem. With this approach, we can solve complex problems more effectively than with the traditional linear approach. Now, more than ever, we need a mindset that looks at the underlying causes, rather than just the symptoms.

The late Gregory Bateson was the pioneer of holistic thinking. An anthropologist, social scientist, and linguist, his work spanned many disciplines. The founders of Neuro Linguistic Programming (NLP) based much of their work on the work of Bateson. He believed that our Western scientific way of thinking was out of line with how nature and our universe solves problems. I agree. We need to learn to think from a holistic and ecological perspective. If we do that, many societal issues will solve themselves.

"The major problems in the world are the results of the difference between how nature works and how people think."
Gregory Bateson

Chapter 5

Why The Need for Human 4.0?

The Fourth Industrial Revolution is more than a technological shift; it's a cognitive revolution.

Any system or organisation can only change if the individuals within it change. Organisms can only change if their DNA changes. DNA carries all the genetic information that determines every trait and characteristic or an organism. In nature, as genetic mutations happen, those changes to DNA leads to changes that allow the organism to better adapt to its environment, and to survive and reproduce. Subtle changes over time allows cells and entire organisms, from the smallest bacteria to complex mammals, to evolve and change.

We need to learn from nature.

If each of us maintain the same DNA of our thinking, we will keep fighting the system until we return to our comfort zone. But here's the catch. What we are fighting for isn't there anymore. It's this fight for the status quo that causes most change programs fail. With so much effort put into fighting for the familiar (even if it wasn't optimal), little energy is left for growth and change. Yet growth and change is a fundamental principle of nature. That applies to individuals, technology and to organisations.

Surprisingly, nature, organisations and technology evolve in following similar patterns. Understanding them is fundamental to understanding what's coming next and how to plan for your future.

Organisations are living entities too. They only change if their DNA changes and they can only change on the outside by changing on the inside first. The DNA of any organisation is the language and unconscious habits that prevail inside it. It's only when they change that the organisation can adapt and thrive.

We need to recognise the real importance of individual people inside our larger systems. Only then can we create organisations and technologies better adapted to the coming challenges. By applying the principles of biology and evolution to the study of organisations, we can develop new technologies to support us.

I have discovered the patterns of how technology moves to the next evolutionary wave. The principles of biology can help us create a more resilient and adaptive world where technology and organisations can play a major part in helping us all to thrive.

Transitioning From Human 3.0 to Human 4.0

Focusing on our inner world will help us adapt to the huge shifts already happening. It will play a major part in reducing the negative stress that we are all feeling. The pressure and disruptions happening now are a potential springboard for our personal growth and transformation. The shift from human 3.0 to human 4.0. is no longer optional.

We need to reconsider how we think, act, and interact with ourselves, others, and the rest of the world and cultivate greater awareness, empathy, and compassion, embrace decentralisation, self-organisation, and collaboration. We must let go of old ways of thinking and doing, and create a new reality based on higher consciousness, purpose, and values.

We all need a sense of purpose and meaning to help us to stay motivated and focused on a long-term vision of a better world. The massive population shifts and dislocation of communities reveals what happens when a sense of purpose and meaning is missing - it brings misery and conflict.

We need to help more people find what they are looking for. But here's the rub. We haven't been trained to know where, or how to look for what brings out the best in us. We would benefit from more democratic and participatory structures in our communities, governments, and organisations so that decision-making is shared and that power is distributed more evenly.

The gap that's growing between the most powerful and least powerful is unsustainable. We have to find a better way.

Chapter 6

The Traditional 3.0 Mindset and Worldview

The linear and predictable world is gone. It's now volatile, uncertain, complex, and ambiguous -- a VUCA world. The skills and knowledge guaranteed success have been replaced by machines that outperform us. Our reliance on rigid structures and hierarchical problem-solving no longer serves us either. The very foundation of how we think, work, and live, is shifting daily.

Let's flip the coin over. The disruption is an opportunity because although machines excel at logic and efficiency, they can't replicate the depth of human creativity, empathy, and adaptability.

We need to confront the limitations of the traditional 3.0 Mindset we have grown up with. How has this mindset has influenced your life? Have you felt the need to follow a set path, or to measure your self-worth by your external achievements? Have you ever hesitated to change because it felt safer to stick with what you know?

These are the hallmarks of a 3.0 worldview that prioritised stability over adaptability, control over collaboration, and logic over intuition. What if, instead of clinging to the old ways of thinking, we embraced a new mindset that values adaptability, creativity, and purpose?

It won't be easy. Letting go of deeply ingrained habits and beliefs is always going to be uncomfortable. But worth it. Humans are remarkably resilient and resourceful. We've adapted to major shifts before, from the agricultural revolution to the digital age. We have the opportunity to do it again, this time with a deeper understanding of what makes us uniquely human. We just need a map. Before we can comprehend the magnitude of the technological storm ahead, we must first understand the inner landscape it will sweep across. Every external disruption mirrors an internal one. As our technologies evolve exponentially, so must our perception, awareness, and emotional capacity. The Fourth Industrial Revolution is not just reshaping our systems; it is rewiring our nervous systems, our values, and our sense of meaning. The real revolution begins not in code, but in consciousness.

Chapter 7

The Great Disruption

How Technology is Reshaping the World

It wasn't so long ago that our world was no bigger than our eyes could see, and no bigger than our feet could carry us. We lived in small communities where small local changes often took several generations to become visible. Things were relatively stable and predictable.

But today in our unstable and unpredictable world that's globally connected through technology, when something happens on one side of the planet, we know about it on the other side almost instantly. Significant changes don't take generations to make an impact. Shifts are seen in months, weeks, or even days.

Every day, we see new breakthroughs that we didn't dare dream of just 2 years ago. The convergence of AI, quantum computing, robotics, big data, and advanced sensors make new economies possible. And we are nowhere near the peak of these advances, they're only just beginning. As a futurist I see the next 5 to 10 years looking something like this.

A tsunami of radical change is coming at us at unimaginable speed. A tidal wave of digitisation, automation, and disruption will soon destroy many old systems and organisations. People can see the wave coming and it's causing a great deal of stress. They know something is about to hit, they just don't know what, or when.

Imagine lying in the water looking out to sea and seeing this enormous wave coming at you. Whether you are in a small yacht or a huge tanker, you know that it's so big that it's going to engulf you. You'd be asking yourself if you will survive, or if you'll be lying on the seabed. The ship's captain, helmsman, or the sailor would all experience the same stress. That's what's going on inside organisations today. People are looking out the window and they can see the tidal wave coming, and they have no idea what to do.

Leaders don't know which way to navigate, investors are in new territory, politicians don't know whether to turn left or right to survive. Managers question if their department is still relevant, directors and shareholders wonder if their companies can change course fast enough.

Employees worry about the safety of their jobs and the relevance of their skills. Millions of people are asking if they are going to survive.

They are scary times, but the good news is that there are people and organisations with a different perspective. They see the wave as a huge opportunity. It is a matter of perception and mindset.

Those who are ready to adapt have the mindset of a surfer. They know just when and where they need to be to utilise the power of the wave and turn it into exponential progress.

We know most of these organisations because we have their products in our pocket. They are the apps on our smartphones that won millions of customers within a few short years because they developed a new, easy-to-use user interfaces that helped people to manage life's complexities.

If you have always been told that big waves are dangerous and that you must stay away, your first reaction is stress, not innovation. Under stress, your pre-frontal and neocortex brain switches off, and the autopilot of your primitive brain kicks in. You go into fight, flight or freeze mode.

In fight mode, you resist and try to stop the wave. In flight mode you run faster, but it won't be fast enough. If you freeze and do nothing, you get swept away. But if you've been told that waves are a fascinating natural phenomenon can work for you, your reaction is more likely to be to ask how you can use its power for a great surf experience. Same wave, different experience.

People who embrace waves conduct themselves differently; they study wave patterns, know exactly where and when they will start to swell, and then jump on to pick up speed. Maybe things don't go well the first few times they try, but gradually, they get better at learning to anticipate the wave and to jump on at the right moment.

Technology simply helps people manage complexity. The better the technology does that, the more disruptive the effect. For example, consider Apple's iPad, it's easy-to-use and intuitive; children, the elderly, and people with disabilities can enlarge their world because they can communicate better with their environment with an iPad. It's creator, Steve Jobs, said, "Disruption is all about identifying new user interfaces".

The big elephant in the room is that disruption is not about technology itself. Disruption is about humans, their behaviour, and their needs. The purpose of technology is to empower human beings and enable ordinary people to do extraordinary things. Yes, we use technology to do things, but it's really about serving people's needs.

"Technology is all about enabling ordinary people, to do extraordinary things"

Steve Jobs

Jobs understood that technology is just an 'enabler' to help people do things they couldn't do before. The more a new interface allows people to manage complexity, the more disruptive it is, and the greater its disruptive effect on traditional systems. It's all about user interfaces.

In the late 1960s, the foundation of the internet was laid with ARPANET, a network designed to share information between select institutions. While groundbreaking, it was far from user-friendly, it was more like deciphering a secret code. Computing was complicated, time-consuming, and reserved for a select few. The internet was powerful network connecting researchers and universities, but it was a mystery world hidden behind technical commands and text-based interfaces. Then in 1989 the visionary Tim Berners-Lee proposed the World Wide Web. In 1993, Marc Andreessen and Eric Bina developed Mosaic, the first web browser to combine text and images in a graphical interface. Suddenly you could see colourful pictures alongside text and you could click on links to navigate, like turning the pages of a magazine. Mosaic transformed the internet into a place where visuals and simplicity invited more people in.

Take a moment to reflect on how a simple shift toward user-friendliness led to massive change. The transformation of the internet teaches us that when technology becomes accessible, it empowers individuals and fuels progress. Every significant advancement begins with a small step towards inclusion and understanding.

Another user interface revolution was the touchscreen smartphone. Less than 20 years ago accessing information meant being tied to a desk, staring at a bulky computer with endless wires and little portability. Laptops were better, but they were still bulky and you couldn't look at it while you were waiting to be served in a cafe. Then Apple launched the iPhone with a revolutionary new interface. It was an easy-to-use computer that you could carry it in your pocket and allowed you to effortlessly manage complex tasks, access unlimited music and get online anywhere.

Smartphones spread like wildfire. As the devices were transformed, our everyday lives did too. Take a moment to reflect on how that shift impacted you. Maybe you now easily navigate new cities, stay connected with loved ones, or learn new skills on the go. The smartphone didn't just shrink the computer; it revolutionised how we interacted with the world.

The next big technological interface has already presented itself: Artificial Intelligence.

The rise of AI has already produced some of the biggest shifts so far, and the pace of change is astonishing. Just two months after the introduction of ChatGPT, version 3.5, in November 2022, 100 million people were already using its new AI. It's one of the fastest adoptions of technology ever.

The current AI wave will have twice the impact of the whole internet in half the time.

There's a pattern behind all of this that I discovered it in 2013. It has totally changed my perception of the future and it can help you ride the wave. I have made it my life's work to decode the pattern and translate it into a model. Over a decade later, that model can help you to view the changes positively and embrace the future, no matter how radical it may be.

Chapter 8

The 4th Industrial Revolution and Our Brains

Machines not only think faster that we do, they learn faster too. AI can predict our needs before we do, and the boundaries between the physical, digital, and biological worlds blur into one seamless reality. But what does this mean for our brains?

Our brains are incredibly adaptable. Like a muscle that grows stronger with use, our brains have a remarkable ability to rewire themselves in response to new challenges and experiences. The brains' ability to literally rewire itself is known as neuroplasticity. It allows us to learn new skills, adapt to new environments, and even integrate cutting-edge technologies into our daily lives. Think of it as upgrading your brain's "software" to keep up with the demands of a rapidly evolving world.

Today, the constant influx of information strains our attention span, and digital tools may alter the way we store and recall memories. So, how can we adapt our minds to thrive in a VUCA (Volatile, Uncertain, Complex, and Ambiguous) environment?

The dramatic and high velocity shifts we are experiencing need an entirely new approach to mindset, thinking, and problem-solving. It helps to understand the thinking patterns that creates that stress for people. The effects of stress chemicals like cortisol and adrenaline are cumulative, meaning they get pumped into your body much faster than it can remove them. What takes a few seconds to put it, takes hours to dissipate. Every little stress trigger stacks chemicals one on top of the other. This doesn't help us to perform at our best, but by understanding a little about the process, you can better manage your cognitive performance.

When people are operating in a stressed state, our evolutionary reaction is to fight against change and show stiff, rigid, and automatic behaviours. That's why the VUCA world causes us long-term chronic stress.

The fear of change will not help us solve the problems we face today. We need to move to a mindset that's more focused on the here and now, so we can tap into the present moment, rather than be overcome by the fear and stress that's dominant for most of us.

It's a sad fact that throughout our lives we are more and more conditioned to a certain way of thinking. Formal education, religions, science, the media, and governments tell us how to think and even what to think. Our brains are being both consciously and unconsciously conditioned by information coming at us at almost every waking moment. By breaking that cycle of conditioning, we have the opportunity to open up new perspectives and opportunities.

During our lifetime, we are increasingly forced to put our minds in cognitive mode. Traditional paths of study may allow us to become doctors, lawyers, scientists or professionals in our field, but they can block our thinking in the process. The more we think this is normal, the more familiar we find it, and the less open and open-minded we can become. It's not our fault, it's how our brains work, because they are amazing pattern recognition machines.

Humans look for patterns in everything. Everything we see or hear is automatically labeled and put in a box of associated memories based on rules and principles have been defined for us by other people. This automatic response was useful in a slowly changing world, but it's not useful in the world we live in now. It will be even less useful in the future.

We need more people who can look at things in a childlike and holistic way. People who can come up with creative, out-of-the-box solutions, who aren't stuck in patterns or structures determined by the established order. We need novel solutions in companies, governments, energy, medicine, technology, transport finance, to name a few.

Our educational systems, economics, and the scientific world reserve greatest praise for the rational mind. But instead, we should be using our rational mind as a servant of our intuition. We often do our thinking the wrong way around. We need to rediscover and trust our intuition.

Chapter 9

Disrupt or Die

How to Survive in the Age of Digital Transformation

Have you ever experienced a point in your life where you wanted to do things differently, but your old habits prevented you from changing? Maybe you tried to quit smoking, take more exercise, live a healthier life, take a different job, or make more time for your kids. If you made the decision but struggled to make turn the intention into new habits, then you know how hard it is. Implementing good intentions is more difficult than you first thought. That's not surprising, because our habits are recorded in the neural pathways of our brains.

Think of these neural pathways as deeply ingrained cart tracks. Without us noticing, we are constantly pulled back into the old tracks over and over again. Millions of neurons connected to form the pathways that fire your thinking patterns, your nervous system and your muscles so you can move and carry out specific tasks. Our brains form highways for the things we do most. Things like driving a car or making hot drink can be done on autopilot. When you do something you only do occasionally, the neural pathways are fewer and the connections are weaker. Instead of a highway, the route is more like a little used footpath. It's slower going and you have to think about each step while your brain fires the right signals to help you get the task done. So what does your brain do? It looks for a pathway that's already there. It tries to head you back onto the highway. That's why habits are so hard to break.

It's often it's better to make radical changes, but that's not a natural thing to do. Radical changes are usually preceded by a radical change of mindset or perspective. We've all heard stories where a single moment in someone's life became a turning point and was the catalyst for a radical shift.

In 2002, I founded a technology company to help organisations drastically accelerate their pace of innovation. We had large organisations as clients; energy companies, banks, and large retail brands. They hired us to help them think and behave differently. They often knew that their current business model wouldn't survive in rapidly changing times, so the leadership were highly motivated to change. But we quickly discovered just how difficult it is to make radical changes in culture, or products and services inside the walls of traditional organisations.

Every organisation has habits and a similar response to change; in the same way the human immune system works. When cells in the human body (or people inside an organisation) sense something unfamiliar, killer cells are sent to destroy the unknown pathogen. It's a natural reaction. In our company, we had to find our way around that. So, our solution was to facilitated an external incubator for our clients. It was set up like a separate small startup outside the walls of the organisation so they could create a new culture and technology. It worked 8 times out of 10, but we still saw cases where things flipped back to old familiar behaviour. When we studied why, it became clear that it was fear of the unknown; fear of new processes, products, services, markets, or all of the above! It all came down to the fear of change.

The reptilian brain of these organisations were experiencing stress. They went into a fight, flight, or freeze mode that put a stop to the intended change. The likely outcome was they were going to face their own downfall even faster than they expected. I didn't understand it fully at the time. If you know that your current business model is finite and your habits will be your downfall, why would you still fall back into them? Logically, I knew that fear could push people back into old habits, but I only really understood it when it happened to me.

It is 2012. I'm sitting with my wife in a dimly lit hospital room with that typical smell of disinfectant. In the distance, you can hear the beeps of medical surveillance equipment. Suddenly, a female doctor comes in and sits down in front of us. Dressed in a typical white coat with a stethoscope around her neck, she gives us the news. "Mr. and Mrs. Kromme. I'm sorry to have to tell you this, your daughter's health problems are more serious than we first thought. We've just completed her heart surgery with many setbacks, and we believe that her heart problems are caused by a rare genetic disorder found in only a handful of children in the world who all, unfortunately, died a few months after birth. There is no easy way to tell you this, but her condition is incurable. We have decided that your 3-month-old daughter has a terminal diagnosis, so we have to follow protocol. You should know that we will not resuscitate her if she deteriorates, and she is no longer entitled to a new bed in the intensive care unit."

What do you do as parents when they tell you such a thing? What would you do? Would you agree to such a diagnosis, and just take it as red that the doctors were right?

We were afraid of losing our daughter. We experienced huge levels of stress. We were reliant on a traditional medical system based on a specialised and isolated way of thinking. One that only looked at tissues, organs, and symptoms; a system that couldn't help us. But we had no other choice, at least that's what we first thought.

Our first step to radical change was to refuse to accept the diagnosis. We went against the better judgment of teams of academic and medical specialists. We wanted a second or third opinion. There had to be someone who could help us, surely. Maybe there was a different hospital somewhere in the world with a different outlook?

Three months later, sitting on the side of my daughter's hospital bed reading yet another book on holistic health, and I could suddenly see it! WOW. I think I have the answer!

"Look, I know you are the doctor, but I have a book here that's given me insight into how to save our daughter. I want us to try this, or at least give it a chance."

"I'm Sorry, Mr. Kromme, your daughter is our responsibility, and we cannot allow new treatments or therapies within our hospital."

"What do you mean you can't allow it? You know what, I've just made my decision. I know this hospital is a safe environment medically, but it is also without hope. Your intention is not to make her better.

This new therapy offers opportunities, and you are not even willing to try! I think our daughter deserves better than that. If you don't treat her here, we will look for a solution to treat her at home and find people to help us. There has to be a way!"

So, after three months in hospital, we left the medically safe (but hopeless) environment behind, and exchanged it for a medically unsafe (but hopeful) environment at home. Our home became an intensive care unit with nurses, medical devices, and medication. We had to become medical specialists ourselves so we could take care of her. We started the newly discovered treatment, and after only 3 treatments, we saw a huge improvement in her health. We continued the treatments, and in the end, it saved her life.

In 2025 our daughter Lieke is doing great. She is almost 15 years old, goes to school, and leads a very normal life. After a struggle, the doctors have declared her healthy. After much discussion and a lot of negotiation, they have lifted her terminal diagnosis, making her entitled to life-saving surgery again, should she need it.

The doctors now call our daughter a non-scientific child. But, of course, we know better. Many people asked me how we discovered something the doctors didn't know. My answer is always the same. The western medical system is fully specialised and divided into sub-subcategories with separate medical branches with specialists for each type of tissue or organ. We forget to look at the bigger holistic picture. Because of a different perspective, I was able to find a solution that doctors could never have found.

After months of intensive research, I developed a totally new and holistic view of health. I realised that living cells are just like people; they solve problems in the same way and order as people do. And the deeper my research became the more parallels I saw between organisms and organisations, and between biology and technology. It was remarkable.

These insights not only saved Lieke's life, they gave me unique insights into how nature solves problems holistically. A different perspective can literally and figuratively mean the difference between life and death: between surviving and thriving.

Sometimes extreme events are needed to embrace a new perspective. We humans are generally lazy when it comes to change. We will only change if we experience pain and discomfort for a long enough, or if there's simply no other way out of a bad situation.

This is the main reason that many organisms and organisations continue to do what they do, even though they know it can mean their demise. For example, we only stop smoking when we have serious health problems, and we only lose weight and live healthier lives when we get too fat and feel sick. Or as an organisation, we will only develop a new product or service when a new competitor enters the market with something better and cheaper. This behaviour is deeply ingrained in organisms and organisations and when uncertainty, fear, and stress hit, we fall into old patterns.

Brains and organisations love patterns. They are predicable, and have a level of perceived safety. Your thinking brain doesn't have too much say in the matter; until there's a radical shift in perspective. I'm convinced that developing a new perspective is the key to changing your actions in time to get a different result. You just have to ensure that that new perspective (vision, mindset) is so strong that it gives you the strength to break out of the cart tracks.

In the hospital, I was so convinced of my perspective and vision that it gave us the strength to break with the old system and to take our daughter out of hospital and try a different way of healing - against medical advice. I absolutely do not encourage ignoring doctors' advice, but in our case, it was our only option.

What happened in that hospital room wasn't only about medicine; it was a living metaphor for our times. Humanity, too, lies on the edge of a diagnosis made by its own creations. We can choose to remain patients of an outdated system, or become active participants in our own healing and future. Just as we discovered that cells can reprogram themselves through their environment, we can reprogram our relationship with technology. The shift from mechanical to meaningful innovation starts in the same place healing does, with awareness, trust, and connection.

Chapter 10

Seeing The World Differently

A Roadmap for Humanity Inspired by Nature

My search for a cure for a supposedly incurable health issue, gave me the gift of seeing the human body completely differently. A change of perspective can give us all a new way of looking at things, and this is the key to understanding how our world is going to change with the roll out of AI.

When we were searching for solutions for our daughter (rather than just focusing on the problem), I quickly realised that answers wouldn't come from the conventional view engrained in us. At first, I saw a body as the doctors did; a collection of organs connected by different tissues with many complex processes going on within each part. Instead, I started to see the body as an advanced society of billions of cells organised more like a swarm that behaves as one super-organism.

Our amazing biological society of cells, which we collectively call our body, has managed to solve all the problems that our technological society has yet to solve. It is a treasure trove of information and knowledge that can teach us so much, we just need to know where to look, and how to look, at the miracle of nature.

When you consider the natural history of life on earth, in evolutionary terms humans arrived very recently. We have been here for the blink of any eye, but the cells we are made up of have been here for billions of years.

It's these teachings that I use decode and apply to understand how we solve problems going forward. My daughter's rare genetic disorder first sent me studying traditional genetics. Based on genetic determinism, traditional genetics proposes that the genetic information inside the cells you are born with are static and your genetic code remains the same from birth until the day you die. Well, this wasn't giving me the encouraging news I was looking for.

If I had stopped my research with that point, we couldn't have changed much about our daughter's prognosis. But then I stumbled upon the term epigenetics, a relatively new scientific perspective with a more holistic view. It proposes that genetic material in cells continuously adapts to changing environmental factors, suggesting that cells can switch genes on and off based on information from their environment. This fascinated me, so I started avidly reading, and one writer in particular caught my imagination.

Bruce Lipton, an American doctor and cell biology specialist, has extensively researched stem cells and the communication between cells. While cloning stem cells he made a remarkable discovery. He placed genetically identical cells in three different culture trays, then made one change; the environment. What happened was this. The cells in the 1st container grew muscle cells, the 2nd container next grew bone cells, and cells in the 3rd grew fat cells. He showed that genetic information in our cells develops differently based on their environment. Stem cells are born blank, and based on their location can become whatever their environment demands of them.

In a way, people are also born as a blank sheet. They choose a role based the needs of their environment. One person becomes blacksmith and makes tools, another becomes a carpenter and builds houses, another a farmer and grows food. I believe that the environment in which a person or cell is located and grows up in has a massive influence on that person's or cell's formation.

That insight turned my image of genetics completely on its head. It gave me hope because there really was a possibility to steer cells' development and their genetic information. By changing environmental factors, cells could change the behaviour of certain genes by turning elements of their gene expression on or off.

Fascinating as this was, it was at odds with what the doctors were telling us about traditional genetics, but I persisted with my research.

Lipton also showed that if you put a few diseased cells between a majority of healthy cells, the diseased cells recover. But if you put healthy cells between a majority of diseased cells, the healthy cells become diseased. And as my research continued, and I discovered that cells communicate with their environment in a much more advanced way than I first thought. It's connected to the future of technology too, as will become clearer as we progress.

Cells communicate with each other through their outer membrane. Imagine for a moment that a cell as a kind of computer, and its cell membrane is the keyboard. By entering a different input on the keyboard, the cell is programmed differently. Now, that might sound a bit strange, but we humans do exactly the same. Through our skin (our external membrane) we communicate approximately 85% of the information with our environment in the form of non-verbal communication through the expression of emotions, facial expressions, body language, and even our hormones. We can literally smell fear. Even our choice of partner is influenced by body pheromones. We might not be consciously aware of all of this, but our subconscious mind is.

Cells can move between two extreme states, just like we can. In a stressed state, the outer membrane of cells harden, and they reduce their communication with their environment and with neighbouring cells. Information can't readily get in or out through the cells' wall. People do the same under threat, we lock our doors and stop communicating with the outside world and we are far less open to information coming in. At a cellular level, our stress state causes communication problems too and all kinds of processes in our organs and tissues are disrupted. Eventually, this results in problems in our tissues, organs, and finally the whole body. That's the beginning of chronic disease.

The other extreme is the state of relaxation, here the cell membrane becomes thinner and more fluid. It starts to share more information with its environment and with neighbouring cells. Communication channels open and information flows in and out. They become more creative, more innovative, and solve complex problems. This the self-healing capacity of our body - and it's very powerful. Our body has a remarkable ability to repair itself, but we need to enable it by relaxing and taking in good nutrients.

People exhibit the same behaviours as cells in stress mode. They turn inwards and reduce communication with the environment and their colleagues. Collaboration processes suffer, and teams, departments, and eventually, the entire organisation experiences problems. In contrast, when people are relaxed, they communicate freely. They share more information and teams become more creative and innovative and solve bigger problems.

Just like our bodies, organisations can self-heal too, but the conditions that make this possible include having an open, creative and relaxed environment where people communicate, and where they are able to make mistakes and learn from them without blame. The entire culture needs to allow that.

Based on these insights about cells, we found a new kind of therapy that helped our daughter relax at a cellular level. We were able to re-activate her body's self-healing capacity, and step by step her body started to heal itself. It created a cell culture in her body that had a positive effect on her cells' gene expression and today we don't need the therapy anymore. Lieke is almost 15 years old and leads a normal life.

However, this wasn't the end of my research, and for the last 15 years I have been working on how we can use these principles every day. With my background in corporate organisations and technology, I see more and more parallels between how communities of cells solve problems, and how communities of people with technological systems solve organisations' problems. The parallels are astonishing.

Cells are just like people, they are social, they communicate, multiply and start communities. As communities grow larger and more complex, they encounter all kinds of practical problems. They have had to solve the problems first before they can develop further into the next phase of their civilisation. Nature has already solved problems elegantly and intelligently while humans are still grappling with them. Nature offers us a detailed roadmap towards a future regenerative society. The only thing we have to do is follow the roadmap and realign with nature..

"In reality, a cell is a biological mini-me compared to the human body. A cell has every biological system that you have"
Bruce Lipton

So, we have more in common with cells than we initially thought. Cells have been here on earth for billions of years, so perhaps it would be wise to learn from them. They have a lot of lessons to teach us. Nature and technology are not separate forces; they are expressions of the same evolutionary impulse. What we build with silicon and software follows the same adaptive principles that life discovered through cells and DNA. By decoding how nature solves complexity, we gain a roadmap for how our technologies, and our societies, will evolve. The seven waves that follow are not just technical phases; they are the evolutionary heartbeat of intelligence itself, whether biological or artificial.

Chapter 11

From Cells to Sapiens

The Evolution of Technology and Biology

The driving forces of organic life give us the blueprint for how technology has developed until now, and how it will develop in the future. These patterns are predicable, and give us a vision for the future that appears when we understand what nature is telling us. This understanding is not a biology lesson, it is THE foundation to understanding AI and where it's going to take us.

Nature has an incredibly clever way of solving problems, though each solution she comes up with creates a new natural problem to solve. That's because each new solution creates a new level of complexity and sophistication that is the source of yet another new problem. And so it goes on in waves; problem - solution - new problem - new solution - new problem.

In total there are 7 waves of problems and solutions that happen before a whole new layer of complex life, intelligence or technology emerges. After that, the 7 waves start all over again. So, let's explore how that predicable pattern emerges and how it works.

First, there's a survival and cultural problem to solve: a cell survives, divides, and multiplies into larger and more advanced multicellular organisms, facing logistical challenges. Then, it realises it needs a reliable energy system and infrastructure to transport resources from the outside world to different internal parts of the organism. Once these basic problems are solved, an information problem arises: how to adapt to the environment and decide which systems receive what resources, and when they need them.

Fast-growing companies experience similar problems in the same order. With these basic problems addressed, a new problem emerges: automation. How can an organism (or organisation) automate more systems to avoid overusing its capacity, focus on basic functionality, and accommodate more sophisticated functions?

That in turn creates a social problem, how does it interact with a wider community and environment to thrive and grow? Again, our organisations have the same problems at this stage in growth. Nature solves that with communication, and yet again creates another problem. How can it to deal with the complexity of a bigger and more advanced group? That's a planning and reasoning problem. I'm sure you can see the stages and the parallels already.

I'll use practical examples of problems and solutions in both nature, technology and organisations, but for now, let's summarise how nature works things out. The basis of everything going forward is based on these natural laws. Now you have the big picture, let's take a first look at the 7 waves.

1 - Interaction

The first wave is about interaction. At the beginning nature's first wave there were only single cells. The problem they faced a was a simple survival one. To improve survival rates, cells started basic chemical and electromagnetic communication with each other, then clustered into groups to form larger organisms. They became better at gathering food and survival rates increased again. The survival problem was partially solved, but now they had a new problem; logistics. Now it needs ways to distribute nutrients around the system and to get rid of waste. By growing larger, nature had created a distribution problem!

2 - Infrastructure

The infrastructure (the larger organism) evolved to solve the problem of low survival rates. The logistics problem was solved within by developing vascular and digestive systems. That allowed resource distribution and waste removal. Nature created an ecosystem adapted to the environment. By creating distribution systems nature had created a new problem; an information problem. The organism now had the capacity to distribute resources, but how to know where resources were needed, and when?

3 - Information

Nature's solution was the evolution of senses and nervous systems to detect internal requirements across different parts of the organism - and at the same time improve the efficiency of gathering or hunting food in the outside world.

Then, you guessed it, that information solution brought a new problem; how to differentiate between a cooperating organism and food? Nature's solution was to use the senses created to recognise food and avoid and repel predators, and improve reproductive success. But this resulted in another problem, at a certain point there was so much information moving through the nerves and senses that it became tough for the organism to process it all. Now there was the need for instinct and automation.

4 - Instinct

Nature progressively automated more internal processes, allowing it to concentrate more on the external world and enhance food gathering skills and hunting behaviour. This was achieved by hardwiring instincts into brains and nervous systems. What we refer to as the reptile brain today (we all still possess a level of reptilian instinct that safeguards us) provided early creatures with an automated system for biological stability and improved responses to external threats. This automated functionality left room for further development, which stimulated the evolution of more successful but highly selfish individuals. Consequently, there was an increase in socialisation and the advancement of communication systems. A more advanced social brain was the subsequent next step.

5 - Imitation

Like all the waves before it, the imitation wave built on the biological technology built in the previous waves. Organisms were now hardwired to eat and to grow but needed to have more communication skills to make more efficient collaboration possible. To process all that, the mammal or limbic brain developed, creating the cognitive space for the start of more advanced social structures and communities. From here the mammal brain kept developing in processing power and sophistication. But more advanced brains with some level of emotional reactions brought its own problems. If a creature over reacts to every perceived threat in its environment, there's chaos. Energy wasted responding to threats without much rationale. So the foundation for the next level of development was laid.

6 - *Intelligence*

The need to cooperate was now greater than ever. The basic mammal brain started to develop into a more sophisticated machine and the neocortex brain emerged; and great apes and human beings were now possible. With the development of language, humans were suddenly able to become masters of our environment and live in evermore successful societies. Many other species became more successful too as nature solved more problems through this evolutionary wave; apes, dolphins, primates, meerkats and many other species were able to learn faster and faster.

7 - *Imagination*

With the human neocortex developing in sophistication over generations, groups got larger, emotional communication became more subtle and society became more complex. Advanced language emerged and our pre-frontal cortex was increasingly able to consciously manage our creative thoughts and actions, while other parts of our very large brain, manages our day to day survival, without us having to think too much. We don't have to make decisions about breathing, managing our digestive system or thinking about our senses. We take that for granted. With our increased brain power, humans were able to start imagining the future, planning and visualising things that didn't yet exist.

That's the wave we are in now. There are many parallels in nature we can use to enhance our understanding of the waves, how they work, and how they can help us see where we are now, and where we're going in the future.

Chapter 12

Nature's Technology Roadmap

Let's take a tour of the seven wave evolutionary process inside the human body. Surprisingly, there's a lot we can translate from this, that we can use to predict the future.

Our bodies are a complex society of billions of cells, working and living together in harmony. They have the same challenges as human societies do. Cells need food, water, to remove waste, and to communicate with each other. Our body needs to work out which cells have to take priority for our basic needs of survival at any particular moment in time. Our body is a master of logistics, supply chain, waste management, health and communication.

If you want to know where we're going in the future, you first need to understand where we came from. By understanding how biological organisms evolved, you will have a more sophisticated understanding of how technological organisations evolve too.

From the moment I started to see our bodies as a harmonious society of billions of living cells, I started asking questions. What can we learn from a society of cells that is hundreds of millions of years ahead of us? What can we learn from how they live and work together in harmony in large numbers? What can we learn from their ability to solve complex problems? I've been uncovering more natural principles and universal patterns that are useful today.

Our first search for universal patterns begins around a billion years ago. Around then the first single-celled organisms had already begun to cooperate and build larger and more advanced multicellular organisms. I wanted to know how these simple forms of life evolved into an advanced society of cells that formed complex life forms, including us.

When I started looking at organisms from an organisational perspective, and specifically what stages of development they went through, it became obvious that societies of cells were compelled to continually develop new biological systems. It was the only way they could manage complexity and better adapt to their environment. This revealed the 7 **major developmental waves.**

Each wave represented breakthroughs that allowed societies of cells to develop to a higher level, over and over again. At each successive level, cell organisations could cooperate better and improve their chances of survival. As a reminder, the 7 waves are

- Interaction
- Infrastructure
- Information
- Instinct
- Imitation
- Intelligence
- Imagination

Each new wave resulted in a new kingdom of organisms with improved properties and skills. The timescale between each new evolutionary wave becomes exponentially shorter over time. The first waves lasted hundreds of millions of years. The seventh wave covered just tens of thousands of years.

Wave I - Interaction

In the first biological wave, interaction is the main theme. Individual cells developed a primitive form of communication and formed communities, allowing those communities to grow faster. They began building stone-like structures to protect them from the outside world and some of these early structures still survive today. Coral for example. Corals are one of the nature's early lifeforms and its structure was an early prototype for the structure of human bones with a similar structure made from similar material. Corals created their own culture, just like we have with commonalities. There's a cellular language of communication, like a biological set of rules of engagement. Their porous structure enables the cell communities to effectively filter food from the water making more food available, allowing the community to grow faster. Corals have become some of the largest organisms in the world, though their growing size created a new problem. Coral cells mastered the interaction between each other, but needed to get materials from the water and transform them to food and energy for deeper parts of the coral. That's where the second wave came in. Infrastructure was needed and so the next prototype emerged.

Wave 2 - Infrastructure

As organisms got bigger and more complex, the need for good infrastructure grew. Cell communities started to develop digestive systems, organs, and vascular systems needed to convert raw food from the environment into building blocks and energy for deeper cells. They needed logistics systems to transport materials to all corners of the organism. In this wave, worm-like organisms emerge that can transport food through the body by contracting muscles in phases. These structures can be seen as a prototype of our pumping vessels, for example, our intestines and our blood vessels. These new systems enabled cell communities to efficiently take food from their surroundings and transport it to their deeper parts which allowed organisms to grow even faster, which in turn created new, more complex problems. For example, how do you know where food and energy are needed in the community? New problems and challenges arose that the cells had to solve before advancing to the next level of civilisation.

Wave 3 - Information

As cell societies became more complex and larger, organisms developed their own internal information technology. Nervous systems emerged and began to create local nervous systems to solve local problems. Central nervous systems followed, connecting all parts of the cell community allowing communication to happen with speed and efficiency. Later in this wave, sensor systems emerged and became more sophisticated. Sensor systems connected the information from the outside world to the information for the inner world. Systems included antennae, eyes, touch sensors, ears, etc. helping cell communities better adapt to their environment, and increasing their chances of survival once again.

As these new biological information systems came online, more new problems and challenges arose. At one point, so much information was passing over these nervous systems that cell communities were so busy managing it that it limited awareness of the world around them. They needed to automate these information flows so that the focus could be shifted externally again.

Wave 4 - Instinct

In the fourth biological wave they solved the focus problem by developing a brain to manage complexity. Let's refer to it as the reptile brain. Although not confined to reptiles, its function was to automate all internal information processes so that the cell community could shift their focus to increase their awareness of the environment.

The reptilian brain is like a computer central processing unit which connects external sensors (antennae, eyes, and ears) to the internal nervous systems and coordinate everything as a whole. As the reptilian brain became more sophisticated it allowed all kinds of new instinctive routines that allowed organisms to deal with known threats from the outside world. As a result, organisms proved perfectly capable of perfecting their hunting and defence behaviour and finding food, so they got bigger still. The side effect was that it produced organisms with rigid, reactive, aggressive, and instinctive behaviours. Learning new routines was difficult, and it took generations to program adaptations into the reptilian brain. Adapting to the outside world was a slow process. As with the waves that came before it, this brain created new problems because they relied on limited cognitive processing and quick reactions for their survival. Rapid changes of their environment, like a big meteor impact, would endanger the survival of this type of organism. Adaptability was limited.

Wave 5 - Imitation

In this wave, cells developed a new biological system called the limbic brain allowing more social interaction. Often referred to as the mammalian brain, this new technology helped organisms learn faster and adapt more rapidly to their environment. It brought short-term memory helping them to copy the behaviour of others which helped to further improve survival rates. They could also now analyse and recognise their own species, leading to the formation of groups of organisms. For example, herds of mammals emerge where behaviour is copied and more social behaviour is exhibited.

The limbic brain plays a major role in emotional responses related to survival. These emotional, bodily responses are primarily aimed at avoiding danger or obtaining pleasure. Today, we also call this the "pain and pleasure" centres of our own brains. But here, too, problems and challenges arose; too many emotional reactions lead to instability. And evolutionarily speaking, if we keep avoiding pain and seeking pleasure, we don't get very far.

Wave 6 - Intelligence

In the sixth biological wave cells solved this problem with a new advanced system called the neocortex brain. Think of it as a kind of biological AI in the cloud. This powerful brain helps organisms to learn new things and adapt in real-time. This brain enabled organisms to walk upright on two legs and maintain balance, solve more complex problems, develop tools, and develop more sophisticated forms of communication. Better communication skills helped organisms build more complex communities and more sophisticated social systems arose.

Wave 7 - Imagination

Here organisms developed their final biological upgrade, the pre-frontal cortex part of the brain. In humans, this is located in our frontal lobe. It gives us the ability to develop complex communication forms;

language, symbols, and written communication systems. That upgrade gives us the ability to visualise things that don't even exist. We are able to imagine things and understand conceptual and non-tangibles; concepts like gods, religion, government, the state, and money.

But the most important thing the pre-frontal cortex brought us was empathy and self-reflection. This allows organisms to empathise with others and develop desirable social behaviours. It helped us create larger and more complex societies, one that no longer roamed freely and gathered food. We began to create small settlements and villages and develop hierarchical organisation and power structures which developed into the civilisation we know today.

In Summary

This natural pattern gives us a tried and tested roadmap for the future that shows us how we can better adapt to our environment. It also gives us powerful indicators of what the next big developments are likely to be.

"Look deep into nature, and you will understand everything better.

Albert Einstein

Cellular societies have already solved all of society's major problems. If only we could talk to them and ask them about their findings and experience over the past billion years. Well, we can, when we know how to ask! As well as knowing about the pattern, nature also gives us clues for the timing of the next developments. That's where it starts to get very exciting indeed.

Chapter 13

The S-Curve Principle

Why does evolution move through waves? Why isn't it a linear process? When we start looking at the seven evolutionary waves in detail, you see why - and another exciting pattern emerges.

You already know our bodies are highly advanced societies of living cells and throughout the seven evolutionary waves, communities of living cells developed ever newer and advanced biological systems such as tissues, organs, and entire organ systems. Each system has a different function within the larger whole, but all work together toward one goal of being better adapted to their changing environment. The timescales between disruptive waves gets shorter and shorter, yet their impact gets bigger and bigger.

The first biological wave lasted about 400 - 600 million years when not much changed. The seventh wave lasted only tens of thousands of years, yet in that short time everything changed. If you were to measure the time period of the waves on the 12 hours of a clock here's it looks; at 11 hours, 59 minutes, and 55 seconds the Earth would have been virtually unchanged. At 5 seconds to twelve, humans appear, and in the last 2 seconds, we would almost kill our planet.

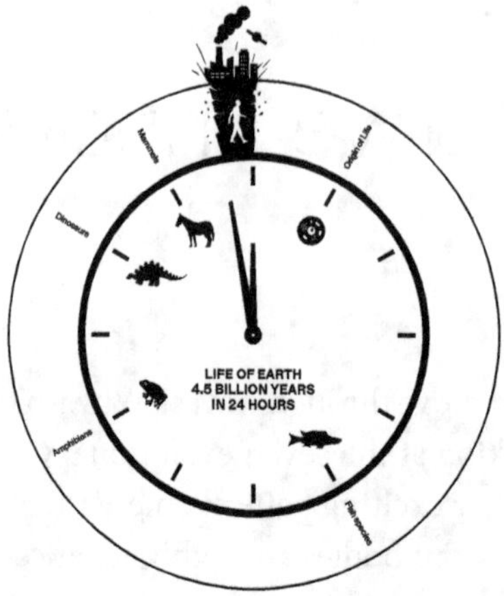

In evolutionary terms, we've only just come along, yet we already have had the most significant impact of all organisms that have come before us.

We are the end product of a long evolutionary process that's taken hundreds of millions of years, but traditional science suggests that the evolutionary process has stopped with humans. I disagree. I'm convinced that the evolutionary process has continued at full speed. If we start looking at it from a more holistic view, you can see that the evolutionary process has continued exponentially. It's just that the process is taking place at a larger scale and speed that's completely outside our traditional mental scope.

We are going through the same evolutionary waves as cells did. Only now, it's not only cells that use biological systems to build organisms, humans use technological systems to build organisations. Although those things might seem far apart, they are remarkably similar. The pattern of development is just the same but the scale is exponentially larger and faster. The building blocks aren't cells, they're humans, we are the new building block of the next phase of evolution.

Humans go through the exact same evolutionary stages, and run into the same type of problems as cells do and we also come up with the same kind of solutions. Let's zoom out and look at the world from above. Humans have gone through several developmental stages, just like the first cells. What's inside us at the cellular level, we also project to the outside. We just don't realise it yet, because we are too focused on our own little world. Our field of vision is simply too narrow.

If we zoom out far enough, we see that humans are just small cells in a larger whole. Cells started in small and remote communities, and so did we. Then we started collaborating on a larger and larger scale, creating more complex organisations. Through our advanced communication skills, we formed larger communities, started trading, and built the society we know today.

When we zoom back in time and look at the individual waves in the evolutionary process the S-Curve pattern found everywhere in nature appears; it starts very slowly, rises exponentially, and then levels off again.

Virtually all new developments (both biological and technological) follow this pattern. They begin very slowly taking a lot of time and energy to make the first small steps in the early stages. Then, as more supporting ecosystems are ready, the development process goes exponentially faster.

Each new S-curve builds a new ecosystem serving as a launching pad for the next phase. Each new eco-system facilitates a new interface to manage the complexity of the previous wave. We see the S-curve at the micro level and at the macro level. It is a nested fractal pattern that repeats itself over and over again. The seven waves are, in fact, connected S-curves, forming a larger S-curve.

Evolution involves shock waves of change that each time provide a quantum leap, suddenly moving change up to the next gear. Pain and discomfort are evolutionarily excellent motivators and applies to both biological and technological evolution. This pattern of radical change is why evolution is not linear.

Cells in an organism only start to change when they experience pain or discomfort for a long time, until they can no longer delay, and then they change en-masse. When mass pain and discomfort are unavoidable, the most significant progress happens, and the S-curve goes up at an exponentially. When it disappears because of the developed solutions, the curve flattens again, and we start the beginning of the next one. This process repeats itself over and over again. These moments of pain are experienced as times of deep crisis.

From cells to sapiens we have evolved through seven S-curves that together form another bigger S-curve. Darwin recognised it. The same principles still apply, as they have done for billions of years.

"It is not the strongest of species that survive, nor the most intelligent, but the one most responsive to change"
Charles Darwin

The organisms best able to adapt to their changing environment are the most successful. Had Darwin been alive today, I wonder if he might have applied his own words to the next evolutionary stage? Would he be saying "It is not the strongest of organisations that survive, nor the most intelligent, but the one most responsive to change."

Chapter 14

From Sapiens To Society

When Organisations Start to Behave like Organisms

We've looked at cells, and we have looked at the human body, so what do cells and homo sapiens have in common? What common evolutionary parallels and patterns are there, and how does it help us to predict the future?

The answer is this. When we see the patterns and know how to interpret them, we know what problems and solutions come next.

The evolutionary process from early humans to the more complex societies we have today, give us a blueprint for how people use technological systems to build organisations.

The universal patterns began thousands of years ago when Earth was relatively quiet and stable. The first homo sapiens started small communities that travelled, gathered food, and hunted animals. Progress was slow at first. The 7 waves in human terms looks like this:

Wave I - Interaction

The agricultural revolution was the first massive technological wave. The interaction between people was the main theme here. Humans developed a more complex form of communication allowing people in early civilisations to interact more socially and to start cooperating in more complex organisations. We used communication to make laws, rules, and conduct commerce and agriculture at scale. Advanced communications allowed the formation of more sustainable and stable organisations that grew exponentially fast. People began building structures in groups; early settlements including villages, and small towns that offered security. Houses kept out bad weather, the village fence and city walls kept dangerous animals and enemies out. Survival rates increased. With agriculture and livestock, communities could obtain food from their surroundings providing more of it allowing those communities to grow even faster.

Accelerated growth brought new challenges for communities to solve. Bigger settlements needed larger amounts of water, energy, food, and building materials and needed to distribute them around the settlement. That was more of a challenge in larger communities.

Wave 2 -Infrastructure

The second wave of technology largely solved logistical problems. For example, the Romans were master road builders. Key Roman land supply routes still survive today. Later, the Industrial Revolution brought the equivalent of the digestive and vascular systems of our society; as communities grew larger, solid infrastructure was needed for a constant supply of energy, water, and building materials. Our ancestors learned that communities with poor infrastructure didn't last long.

People started developing industrial systems and infrastructure to convert raw materials into building blocks and energy. Transport methods became more innovative supplying people in ever-growing communities. Ports, river piers, canals, oil pipelines and railroads emerged, to transport energy and building materials to where they were needed. This happened locally first (paths between villages) and later at a global scale (sea exploration, major ports, cross continental road routes, the silk route between Europe and the Far East). So, communities grew even faster, we had to travel even greater distances, and more new and more complex problems arose.

Wave 3 - Information

It's useful to be able to move people and resources around, but that creates information problems. How do you know where people need building materials, food, and energy, and how do you know where it all goes once it's left the depot? Those new information-related problems had to be solved to advance civilisation. The third wave is about the development of information systems and people began to create solutions using new technological systems. A picture shows the nature/technology parallels more beautifully that words ever can, and you can view it using this QR code.

SCAN FOR MORE

In the lower right corner, you can see the vascular system of an organism, in the main picture, you can see an aerial view of Berlin at night. You can clearly see the functional and visual parallels between homo sapiens and cells, biology, and technology, and between organisms and organisations.

Information systems started slowly, like all S-Curve developments. First, there was the printing press and Pony Express; slow but effective. Information transfer wasn't fast but it could move ideas over long distances. The later telecom revolution brought simple systems like telegraph and telex, then later more complex systems like telephone and fax.

The telecoms revolution brought us the nervous systems that our increasingly large and complex world needed. We could send spoken and written messages over longer distances almost instantly. The development of local telecoms networks was the first step towards solving local information problems, followed by national and intercontinental networks. Communication between supply and demand could take place with greater speed and efficiency. Different sensors, such as microphones and cameras, were developed to enable technologies like telephony, radio, and television. These sensors helped organisations understand what was happening from a distance allowing them to adapt to their environmental needs. But when these information systems arrived, new problems and challenges arose again.

With so much information flowing through the telecom systems, more and more people were needed to manage and process the information (hand-operated telephone exchanges, for example). Now some form of automation was needed.

Wave 4 - Instinct

In the fourth technological wave, new technological systems allowed the automated systems to imitate instinctive behaviours to short-cut decision making. In this wave we developed computers and software to manage and automate complex information processes. Companies like IBM developed the first computer-operated telephone exchanges. These were the precursors of personal computers. Later microchips, control systems and software handled all kinds of intuitive routines. Like the reptilian brain, the computer is a central processing unit connecting external information flows to internal systems of organisations, coordinating everything as a whole.

Computers got faster, more sophisticated, and equipped with all kinds of automatic software routines, managing internal information flows and processes more effectively. As a result, organisations freed up time to focus more on the outside world and do more marketing, sales, innovation, customer support and they scaled up faster as a result.

An unpleasant side effect was that organisations started to exhibit more rigid, aggressive, and instinctive behaviours; the 'computer says no' syndrome. There was less and less human judgement being used and more decisions being made by algorithm. Programming and implementing new processes and routines was difficult, and organisations needed multiple software platform migrations and integrations to learn new functions and skills. Adapting to the real world was a slow process that created new problems related to reptile-like organisations' survival. Rigid and slow organisations both large and small, were just like all other organisms, at the mercy of their environment. Reptile-like organisations were hardwired to eat (make profits) and grow big (dominate) and therefore faced the same fate as the dinosaurs. For the dinosaurs, a meteor came out of space, and for dinosaur companies something unexpected came out of cyberspace. A new environment was coming like a tsunami; the advent of the Internet that would jeopardise the survival of many.

Wave 5 - Imitation

In the fifth wave, problems created by automation were solved with even more advanced technological systems. In the animal kingdom (including us) it was the development of the limbic brain that allowed more complex social systems to happen - and so it was with technology. We developed interconnected systems that allowed social interaction between people across networks. We developed the internet, and in the social media revolution people could exchange ideas and interact more easily. We can compare these networks to the limbic or social brain of organisations and society. This technology helped people and organisations to learn and adapt faster to their environment and to copy successful behaviours of others and learn faster themselves. It helped people to analyse and recognise peers, leading to growing online communities.

Platforms like Facebook and YouTube are good examples. More and more behaviour is copied and social information shared. Almost whatever you want to learn is on YouTube; whether it's seeing what's inside the box of a product, learning how to fix a machine or to start exercising. Currently, many of our systems are running behind the pace of change that this technology has brought into our lives.

Using Big Data and analytics tools, organisations can learn about people's behaviour and respond better to peoples' needs. The Internet and social media now play a major role in public debate about many issues in society. New problems and challenges have come up, from increasing polarisation and fake news that can lead to instability. From politics to animal rights, COVID theories and climate theories; information spreads quickly around the globe. The algorithms of social media platforms are built to stimulate and monetise the pain and pleasure centres of our brain. No wonder extreme polarisation spreads so fast.

Wave 6 - Intelligence

In the sixth wave, people and organisations will be able to largely solve these problems with advanced technological self-learning systems using advanced AI. AI is the equivalent of our neocortex brain for organisations and our society. It will help organisations learn new things and adapt almost in real time, allowing for instant responses to rapidly changing needs and markets, helping us solve extremely complex problems and automate repetitive basic tasks and processes more cheaply.

AI's sensitivity already performs some tasks better than people. For example, recent studies show that AI can detect early-stage cancers years before they become visible to the naked eye of an experienced doctor. AI will continue to develop self-aware organisations that are more aware of their own behaviour. AI can also improve internal and external communication including rapid improvements of advanced dialogue/voice interfaces, real-time translation systems, and emotion recognition. But AI will also create new problems too, many of which will be ethical and moral.

Wave 7 - Imagination

In human terms, this wave goes beyond process and into imagination. In technology terms, the 7th wave will enable us to augment our own imagination and creativity, and transfer that vision to others in a new way. People and organisations will develop holographic technologies and new platforms to enable new levels of collaboration and communication. It will also help us visualise and simulate complex and abstract issues.

The most important thing this new technology can bring is empathy and self- reflection. Holographic devices will allow you to see through someone else's eyes - literally. People and organisations will be able to put themselves into others shoes and develop more social and collaborative behaviour. Co-creation will become more streamlined and rolled out globally. Society will start to behave like a large organism. Just as in biological evolution, the waves' transit time becomes exponentially shorter, and the impact of the wave increases exponentially too.

Think of a large rocket being launched with multiple segments filled with fuel. Each segment gets up to a certain speed, then it disengages and falls away. The segment above builds on the momentum generated by the last segment. Biological and technological waves work in the same way. Each new wave builds on the speed and impact of the previous one.

The Agricultural Revolution took thousands of years, yet the 5th fifth wave (social media) took only 20 years. The 6th wave of AI will only take approximately another 10 years. Each wave has exponentially more impact than the previous one and is a launching pad for the next.

The 5th of the Internet has lasted about 20 years, and in that time a huge amount of change has happened, its impact was, and still is, huge. The 6th wave (AI) will have double the impact of the 5th wave, but last just 10 years.

The 7th wave will take 5/6 years but will have twice the impact of the AI wave. I predict that we will experience 6 times the impact of the internet in the next decade. The impact of the next waves are beyond the current scope of our understanding, and I believe they are being severely underestimated.

So now you understand how closely technology and organisations are subject to evolutionary principles. What I often hear after a keynote is people saying, "But Christian, I don't see technology as something positive at all; just look at the big tech companies like Facebook, for example. They make a mess of things."

That's true if you look at how today's big tech platforms can abuse their power positions and violate ethical and moral issues. Mark Zuckerberg, CEO of Meta (holding company of Facebook) was asked to explain to some of the big data scandals, such as the use of data for election advertising by Cambridge Analytics, privacy issues, and the distribution of fake news to Congress. They understood the problem, but don't have the expertise to police the solution. It's clear that organisations and technology firms are far from perfect. Like all things, they are continuously subject to evolutionary change.

We are experiencing enough discomfort and pain caused by these big tech companies for there to be motivation to trigger change in a direction that serves us once again.

Companies like Apple are already starting to use privacy, morality, and ethics as Unique Selling Points in their marketing. I expect this will be a trend among tech companies in the next 5 to 10 years.

"Humans beings always do the most intelligent thing...after they've tried every stupid alternative and, none of them has worked."

Richard Buckminster Fuller

The self-interests of money, power, and politics drive organisations to make decisions that aren't always the best for wider society. It will stay this way until we collectively experience pain and stop accepting it, then we will steer en-masse in another direction. It's a learning process, during which we become more aware of what we do and what impact this has on our world.

The faster and more powerful technology gets, the quicker we collectively receive feedback and the faster we make mistakes and adjustments. But there is a downside; with a powerful car that goes at 250 kph, if you aren't paying attention, you can run off the road in a fraction of a second. Companies like Facebook have become very big very fast, so we shouldn't be surprised if they are replaced by other organisations contributing more positively to society.

Chapter 15

The Evolution of Technology

We've talked about striking parallels between evolution of nature and technology so now some practical technology examples that illustrate the speed of the progression, and consider where could take us in the future.

We are so surrounded by technological devices that many of them don't even feel like technology anymore. Rewind just 10 or 20 years, and we had large clumsy grey personal computers on our desks that we could only interact with by typing in programming code. That felt very technological! But today, our smartphones and tablets and wearable-like tech, doesn't even feel like tech anymore. Technology has adapted to us fitting seamlessly with who we are, and what we do helping us express ourselves creatively in ways unthinkable a couple of decades ago.

Take the iPad, on the inside it's super high-tech, but on the outside, it feels very natural. You can move objects around the screen with your fingers, draw with a pen, you can talk to it to get it to do things. We can talk to our TV's, operate our central heating through our smart phone while on holiday, and ask our smart speakers to tune into our favourite playlists.

Technology is adapting to our needs and becoming evermore user-friendly because user interfaces are becoming more intuitive all the time as the inside of our devices get exponentially more sophisticated. As we have more computing power at our disposal resolving all kinds of internal complexities, the outside gets more user-friendly.

When we look inside those devices, something remarkable is happening; the chips inside comply with Moore's Law. Gordon Moore, one of the founders of Intel, the chip manufacturer. Moore's law states that every 12 to 18 months, the number of transistors in a chip doubles, so every year you get twice as much computing power for the same amount of money. So, chips evolve along an exponential curve becoming twice as fast year on year.

Traditional desktop and laptops use Intel processors to run the Windows operating system. With the increased power of hardware, the software it can run gets exponentially more powerful too. Take the SD micro-card memory chips in our smartphones. In 2005 you had 128 megabytes on a chip. By 2014 you had 128-gigabytes on a chip for the same amount of money. Just few years down the road, it will be 128 terabytes on a tiny chip, that's a giant leap in less than 10 years. We're seeing the same exponential development in all information processing devices.

Digital cameras are a great example of Moore's Law in action. The first digital camera was developed for Kodak in 1976 by Steven Sasson. It had a resolution of 0.01 megapixel, weighed almost 2 kilos, and cost about 10,000 euros. Digital cameras have become much smaller over the years and at the same time, the resolution has got higher. Today, we have tiny digital cameras that are so small they are almost invisible to the naked eye. Today, tiny medical camera image-chips have resolutions of over 10 megapixels, weigh almost nothing, and cost just 10 euros.

GPS devices have changed our lives too. In the '80s, they were huge and were confined to the defence and offshore industries, heavy and expensive, they were only affordable for large companies. Today we have a GPS chip in our smartphone that are almost invisible to the naked eye. Not only are they tiny, they are much more accurate too with the latest GPS chips transmitting 3D locations to within 10 centimetres accuracy at a fraction of the cost and weigh almost nothing.

Ray Kurzweil, inventor, computer scientist and futurist for Google, was the inventor of text recognition technology and the pioneer of speech recognition. Kurzweil uses Moore's Law to predict where computing is going. He predicted that by 2025, a $1,000 chip will process as many information pulses as the human brain. Whether that has happened or not, or if that comparison is useful, I'm not sure, because I believe our brain is way more complex than a chip. But let's take that comparison for a moment. He calculated that by 2038, for that same $1,000, you will be able to buy a chip that can process as many information pulses as all the human brains on Earth combined. This comparison reflects the exponential growth in computing power coming in the next decade. Just imagine that much computing power inside your smartphone, being able to process as much information as every human brains earth, on a device that fits in your pocket. What would we do with this amount of computing power? What problems will we be able to solve?

Kurzweil named the effect of Moore's Law as the Law of Accelerating Returns. Using faster computer systems, we can make even faster computer systems. Each new computer technology is another stepping stone, a launching pad for the next technology to develop from. In turn, that allows us to go even faster. Moore's law is already outdated because technology is moving even faster than Moore's law predicted.

In the year 2000 scientists were aiming to sequence the DNA of the human genome. That was going to take massive computing power needing gigantic data centres of supercomputers. The team predicted they would need at least 100 million dollars to finish the project, but they were wrong because they didn't incorporate Moore's Law into their calculations. The computing cost went down even faster than exponentially annually. In fact, recently, I read that there is now an accessory that allows you to do DNA sequencing on your smartphone so the price is now almost to zero. In just 20 years, the cost has gone from $100 million to nearly $0.

Although exponential growth and progress are hard for the human mind to grasp, today's rate of change is going even faster than Moore's law. AI chip maker NVIDIA reports that their chips double in performance every 6 to 8 months. That's twice as fast as the doubling by Moore's law. That's an annual quadrupling of computing performance, exponentials on top of exponentials. At NVIDIA's last conference they reported that their AI chips had improved a million times in the last decade. NVIDIA expects that they will at least do another million times improvement in the next decade. Starting from where we are now and increasing todays AI capabilities a million fold goes beyond our cognitive horizon. We simply cannot grasp what this will mean and what it will look like.

Our current computer technology is almost running at its limit. We are nearing the end of its transistor-based chip S-curve. We are probably in the final decade of using transistor-based silicon chips. The next step for computation and data processing is quantum computing. Quantum computers are a whole new generation of computers, offering the potential to go much faster. Google's latest Willow quantum chip has the potential to exponentially reduce errors as it scales up by incorporating more qubits. This breakthrough addresses a critical challenge in quantum error correction that the field has been grappling with for nearly three decades. Moreover, Willow demonstrated remarkable performance by completing a standard benchmark computation in a mere five minutes. This feat surpasses the computational capabilities of the fastest supercomputers of today that would need 10 septillion years to complete the same task. That number is beyond the estimated age of the Universe.

Quantum computers are a completely different computing concept, and how they work is not easy to explain, but let's try anyway. A traditional computer solves problems sequentially. Imagine a soccer field full of hundreds of thousands upside down plastic cups. Under one of them is a ping pong ball and the computers' job is to find it. A traditional transistor-based computer lifts up each cup, one by one. It might find the ball quickly if it's is at the beginning of the field, but if the ball is at the other end, it could take days, weeks, even months to figure out where the ball is. A quantum computer does things very differently. It lifts up all the cups in one go, and immediately finds the ball. It's an entirely different order of magnitude of power, perfectly suited to facilitating and empowering neural networks. It will be a gigantic boost for AI applications.

"The greatest shortcoming of the human race is our inability to understand the exponential function."
Prof Albert Bartlett

Virtually everything in nature, cell growth, population growth, and the network effect all develop exponentially. For humans, exponential growth remains a tricky concept to grasp. We get the idea on a conscious level but our brain can't comprehend the results. The effects of quantum computing is difficult to grasp, but when it becomes mainstream our lives are going to change forever.

Chapter 16

Understanding Exponential Growth

The words exponential growth are easy to say, but their meaning is more difficult to comprehend. To understand their implications on our future, it's essential to grasp what they really mean, because it's going to alter our world in a way that hasn't registered with most people.

Professor Albert Bartlett said, "the greatest shortcoming of our human race is our inability to understand the exponential function". However abstract the concept may seem, the implications are going to affect the everyday life of every single person on the planet.

If I asked you if you take thirty linear steps, you would easily be able to tell me where you would end up, relative to your current location. If I were to ask you where you would be in thirty exponential steps, then you would probably have no idea. Your brain would struggle to even imagine it.

Bartlett, a physicist, researched population growth and its relationship with human energy use. Population growth is subject to an exponential curve, starting on a microscopic scale, and then increasing exponentially. For around ten thousand years human population was fairly stable, then it suddenly spiked sharply upwards. That's the exponential function in action. Once a certain level is reached, it takes fewer and few years to add an extra billion to world population. Each additional billion takes even less time. A doubling that took 700 years in earlier times when population was smaller, now happens in just fifteen years. Then growth peaks, and that's an exponential peak. The numbers are interesting, but still doesn't help the human mind to really comprehend the exponential function.

The Emperor's chessboard tale tells the story of a sage who the Emperor asked what he would want in return for a service he required. The sage said, "I would like a chessboard, and on every square I want grains of rice. One grain on the first square, two on the second, four on the third, eight on the fourth and double the number of grains on each square across the board after that. It sounded reasonable enough, so the emperor agreed. But when his servants started filling up the chessboard, the number of grains of rice went up more quickly that the Emperor had been able to comprehend. They increased exponentially. On the first two rows they could still stack the rice, but after that, it got out of control. They realised that they had to cover the entire country with metres of rice to meet the number of grains to meet the agreement. With exponential growth and the continuous doubling, numbers go up to astronomic heights after a number of doublings.

Imagine a drop of water in your hand that doubles in volume every minute. At one minute, you have one drop. In two minutes, the water volume has doubled, in three minutes it's doubled again. In seven minutes, you have a slightly larger puddle. If you were standing in 50,000 capacity The Yankee Stadium and that first drop of water was in the middle of the field at 12.00 noon and the drop doubled in size every minute, how long do you think it would take to fill the whole stadium with water?

When I'm giving a keynote, I often ask the audience that question. Answers vary from weeks, to months, or even years. In reality it would only take fifty minutes, just fifty doublings, before the whole stadium is filled with water. It takes 45 minutes to get just one metre of water, enough time to grab a hot-dog. One meter becomes two, and the next doubling four meters, eight meters, sixteen meters, thirty-two meters and suddenly the whole stadium is underwater. You have less than 5 minutes to eat your snack, because the stadium will be full in just 5 minutes. We struggle to comprehend the exponential function.

The rising water is a good analogy to understand how computer technology has developed over the past few decades. The first bulky computers got a little faster every year, but changes added up, and became exponential. That doubling continues today.

Today we are at the equivalent of just one meter of water in our stadium. We will soon go to two metres, four, eight, sixteen meters and so on. The pace has reached a critical mass where we are going to really start seeing the impact. That's why I talk about a tsunami, and it's really coming, the doublings keep coming, but how you view it depends on your perspective. Some see a threat, and others see the rising wave as a way to gain huge momentum.

That's exactly what today's disrupters are doing. Companies that look afresh at processes and solutions and use today's advanced technologies, can speed up exponentially. Whether it's a threat or an opportunity depends on your mindset. By looking at technology from a positive mindset you can make a lot of headway, just as the big wave surfers do.

"Trust the exponential, be patient and be pleasantly surprised"
Sam Altman

You can assume that exponential doubling is consistent, and it goes on and on and calculate where the curve goes up. When it does, technology becomes extremely powerful all at once. If you're in the right place, at the right time, all of a sudden, you can be that surfer.

Chapter 17

Welcome to the AI Revolution

AI progression is staggering. In 2024, more than a million robots were deployed in Amazon's distribution centres. The most recent large language model AI systems have over a trillion parameters. Every six to eight months AI model capacity is multiplying between two and five times capability. As the amount of information grows, the speed and of the processing power to use it grows with it.

It would have taken two weeks for two human researchers to dig through PhD papers to augment research and a couple of weeks to read through a hundred patent documents. Now one person can do it alone in 30 minutes using AI.

Even the AI disruptors are being disrupted. The launch of Deep Seek from China showed that training the model itself cost just $3-5 million. Open AI spent $100 million to do the same job, and the operational costs of Deep Seek are fraction of previous AI costs.

Google's MED Gemini AI already outperforms medical experts for accurate diagnosis of many illnesses. Already, 25% of all the code created at Google is written by AI, and it's learning exponentially fast. That percentage is going to grow really quickly.

The first ChatGPT with very basic reasoning level was ranked as the 1 millionth best programmer worldwide. When GPT 01 launched in October 2023 it ranked 9800 of the world's best programmers, then GPT 03 launched December 2024 was ranked number 175 on the list of the world's best programmers. Today, they have an AI model called GPT 5.0. It's already ranked number 50 of the best world's best programmers. By the end of 2025, we will have probably have an AI model in the top 10.

Many IT experts predict that within a few years, AI will be writing 90% of all computer code. Humans will still have to define what the code is meant to achieve and specify the design decisions, so we will still need programmers - but they will have a very different set of responsibilities to grapple with. Our native language will be the new programming language of the future.

With such power at our finger tips almost anyone can create a TV commercial, compose a song, or create a website or app without any coding knowledge at all. For example, a four year old kid could program the next killer app that goes viral. Things that still costs millions of dollars today are going to become a cheap commodity very quickly.

In addition to the exponential growth in speed, accuracy and capability there's another angle. AI is likely to become a firewall for every single one of us. It's going to be filtering what's relevant and what's not. It will be making shopping decisions for us based on what it knows we value. For one person it will be price or ecological friendly shipping methods, for another it will be brand, colour or commercial relationships with others. Soon AI will be making even more decisions for us than it does already. This is going to be easy when AI has an IQ ten or twenty times greater capacity than we have, and it's already on the way.

AI is the foundational layer for the 7th wave. When AI 'understands' the world around us, we can move towards the next interface that's even more intuitive. When AI 'knows' how reality works it can seamlessly integrate the physical real world with the virtual world. The digital world simply becomes an indistinguishable layer on top of our real world.

The technology that is coming in the 7th wave is mind boggling, and will be even more game changing than AI itself. I predict that we are going to move away from 2D user interfaces. The internet will be 3D, visual and presented as a 3D layer that sits on top of our physical reality.

Apple has already developed their Apple Vision Pro headset that uses a spatial operation system so you can navigate apps with your eyes and tell them what to do from your voice, all presented in a realistic 3D environment that matches your natural environment. The Apple Vision Pro and similar devices are a small step towards new spatial interfaces that will replace traditional 2D window interfaces like your smartphone, tablet or laptop. Traditional interfaces will go out of the window.

Next generation user interfaces will, for example, be a photo realistic virtual person that stands next to you. They might be your personal coach, doctor, private banker or mentor. You can interact with this person like a real person to help you develop your personal skills and achieve your goals.

Or how about being able to spend time with a relative or co-worker in Australia without having to get on a flight? Currently these interfaces are expensive, heavy or clunky.

Holographic devices and apps are only at the bottom of their development S-Curve, and you know how quickly those S-Curves ramp up. Developments are slow to get going in the early stages, so everyone underestimates them, then as things ramp up (materials, miniaturisation, chips, power consumption, programming and design) the speed of implementation really takes off. In 5 to 10 years' time we will look back and think how pre-historic the communication and AI tech we are using now was. To put things into perspective, even the smartest AI that you use today will soon become the dumbest AI that you use for the rest of your life.

Chapter 18

The Evolution of AI

All the developments I've outlined were totally predictable using the 7 waves model. So that you can make your own predictions for your industry (or your life), you need a basic understanding of how AI evolves. Let nature help us once again, so you can more fully understand the roadmap.

The development and evolution of emerging technologies are highly predictable. I base my technological predictions on a universal set of solid principles. Both biology and humans follow the same evolutionary patterns; when a certain level of complexity is reached, the next wave of evolution begins.

To better understand AI, or, more correctly said, the synthetic intelligence wave in more detail, we must first understand how natures' biological intelligence works.

Let's use human development as an example. Within seconds of a baby boy being born, his reptile brain (the automation brain), is fully operational. All reflexes are working, and the body can maintain homeostasis. The limbic or mammal brain is also almost fully operational, the baby recognises his mother and father based on the sound of the voice or their smell. The neocortex brain is like a clean sheet of paper. At first the baby starts using their eyes and other senses to make sense of the world and recognise simple patterns, shapes and colours. When he understands the world to a limited degree, he starts to move, first crawling, then walking. At 2 to 3 years old, he starts to understand more complex patterns like simple language. Then, he shows signs of generative intelligence, scribbling and drawing. Then he starts to detect and generate language; first words, then sentences, then coherent stories. Finally, when young adults understand the environmental context and language, they are given more agency and more responsibility, and they start to make decisions.

AI is currently going through the exact same developmental stages, but it learns much faster than humans do. Recently the co-founder of DeepMind and Inflection AI said on X,

"AI is like a new kind of life - a digital species. We need to treat this development with the care we'd give to raising a child."

AI is already better than humans in recognising and interpreting sensor information, complex patterns in images, big data and sensor data and is faster and more accurate. The sheer amount of data it can process dwarfs the capacity of a human brain.

When we put sensors and cameras in a car or drone, AI can already drive or fly better than many humans. Just a few years ago, AI entered its third stage of evolution and started recognising advanced patterns like language. AI can read and speak more than 160 languages, plus 90 programming languages and counting.

By the time this book gets to print that number will have already expanded. AI's large language models are already better than humans in recognising textual information and natural language. Now, AI is entering the fourth stage; generating patterns like complex text in designated writing styles, images, lifelike deep-fake video and audio, and many other complex outputs. Although this Generative Artificial Intelligence sounds new, biology discovered this domain long before human technologies did.

Although recognition of human communication sounds simple, language is highly complex; the meanings of words change constantly based on context, background, culture, and other variables. Very soon, AI will better understand the outside world through the use of sensors and cameras and will understand the conceptual world of language more than it does now. When we give these AI systems more responsibility, they will be allowed to make decisions too. The parallels are striking, just look at the comparisons between human development and the capability of AI:

1) Simple pattern recognition (Perceiving shapes, patterns, colours, understanding the environment)
2) Movement (grasping objects, crawling and walking)
3) More complex patterns (hearing and speaking language)
4) Generating patterns (making drawings, speaking, writing stories)
5) Autonomy and agency (voting for a party and driving a car)

AI is now moving to the fifth stage, meaning it will understand the conceptual and textual world by reading and studying the entire internet. It understands the world by using it digital senses such as cameras and sensors outside the limitations of the 2D internet too. The fifth stage will be one of the most impactful stages. AI will be able to transform many more processes into autonomous ones, and that's going to include large parts of our economy.

The AI S-Curve

AI evolves following the waves and S-curve principles where the curve starts almost flat and developments happen slowly and a lot of energy and money is needed to make it work in the early stages. Then, over time, the eco-systems take shape and developments pick up speed until they are exponential. We are at the beginning of the exponential part of the curve and AI's power and capability will increase dramatically in the next few years.

After the exponential phase, the technology matures, and the curve flattens once again. The technology will still continue to evolve, but the societal and organisational impact will decrease. A good example is the iPhone 13 versus the iPhone 17; the 17 is a better and more advanced iPhone, but the pressure to buy one decreases because the difference in performance is less noticeable for the average user.

With AI, we will see the same pattern. We will struggle to tell the difference between an AI with an IQ of 800 or an AI with an IQ of 1000. In both cases it will be cognitively more intelligent than a person, but the economic pressure to develop ever more intelligent AI systems will decrease as the maturity of the technology increases.

At the beginning of the AI S-curve, simple pattern recognition AI systems recognised patterns in numerical data, short text, big data, sensor data, and simple images. The first S-curve products were mainly data analytics tools and simple chatbots that poorly understood words and sentences with very simple face and voice recognition. There were also the first predictive and prescriptive analytics tools that helped to predict future patterns.

Today, as we are at the beginning of the exponential part of the AI S-curve we see more advanced pattern recognition systems. Large Language Models like ChatGPT, Claude and Google Gemini are evolving exponentially. The more that people use them the 'cleverer' they get. AI systems can now recognise large complex patterns in spoken and written languages as well as programming languages. And because AI is recognising our natural language, it can take its commands from it and translate that into all kinds of commands in programming language. The result is generative AI tools (tools driven by multiple algorithms) that can generate complex texts, advanced images and videos. Natural language has become an essential and new user interface to communicate with advanced technological systems. This is a significant shift; instead of humans adapting to technology, technology has already started to adapt to humans.

Experts predict that the language AI training models will be 1,000 times larger in just three years. The next generation of AI systems will be capable of advanced reasoning, planning, and autonomously completing more advanced and complex tasks. Besides understanding textual information, AI will start to understand the full spectrum of information; visual, sensor, and auditory information. Multimodal AI systems will start to make its own sense of our world.

With that understanding it will make more and more decisions. Starting with simple decisions, such as parts of a business process, later on AI will make more advanced and critical decisions. It won't be long before we see AI managing a medium or large company via AI-powered management or a CEO.

We will probably see AI driving or flying fully autonomous vehicles and managing fully autonomous factories. In some farming and manufacturing environments, we are almost there already. Progress is not measured in years anymore, it is measured in months, and I believe will be even measured in weeks or days. Today's progress will be the slowest you will experience for the rest of your life. Computing power will continue to explode, so you can expect to be able to run advanced AI models and algorithms offline on your smart device using advanced AI computing technology.

There will come a point at which AI will be too limited operating in a digital only space. To become more capable, it needs to experience the real world. We will see more autonomous robots that explore the natural world like we do.

Boston Dynamics, Figure and Tesla already have human shaped robots that can navigate their way around a snowy forest floor even rebalancing in a highly complex and challenging environment. We take being able to walk through a wood for granted, but for a robot it's a highly complex task. By exploring the real world, AI will learn to understand the context of our world compared to the conceptual world and will be able to make even more decisions. The big question is this; what decisions need to be made by us, and what kind of decisions will we allow AI to make?

We are quickly evolving from simple pattern-recognition AI systems to advanced pattern-recognition AI systems that understand context and environment. We are moving from relatively simple generative AI systems like the first versions of ChatGPT to highly advanced generative multimodal AI systems capable of reasoning and planning at an astonishing pace. It's going to have a massively disruptive effect on the very fabric of our society. We stand at the intersection of two accelerating curves, technological progress and human confusion. As AI evolves, it amplifies not only our intelligence but also our uncertainty. The real challenge is not building smarter machines, but cultivating wiser humans. Before we can make sense of the chaos outside, we must find coherence within, aligning our technological power with our emotional and moral maturity.

Chapter 19

Generative AI

Generative AI is going to have a massive impact on both organisations and jobs. New AI startups are emerging daily to address specific problems. AI is more than just a trend, it's a massive transformative wave, much like the internet was a few decades ago, but it is exponentially more potent and happening in a shorter timeframe.

We're reaching a critical tipping point in our interactions with machines. For the past 20-30 years, we've had to adapt to technology by learning to program and operate them. However, now that technology is so much more powerful and intelligent, it's beginning to adapt to us through more user-friendly interfaces so the technology adoption rate is going to massively accelerate.

Consider that ChatGPT-3.5 launched in November 2022. Its creators made huge breakthroughs and within the first two months it had over 100 million monthly users, one of the fastest user increases in history. ChatGPT-4 followed shortly afterwards, boasting an IQ of 114, making it more intelligent than most people. It not only passed nearly all academic exams created for people, it consistently ranked among the top 10% of the best students (ChatGPT 3.4 was positioned in the worst 10% of the students). It was more adept at advanced reasoning and more consistent in its responses. While ChatGPT-4's results were already impressive, it was just the beginning.

Leveraging ChatGPT-4's capabilities, next came Agentic AI's that allowed you to configure and deploy Autonomous AI agents, give them custom names and assigning them any imaginable goal. These agents attempt to reach their goals by devising tasks, executing them, and learning from the outcomes. Agentic AI's applications are limitless and will significantly impact entry-level jobs in the corporate world.

ChatGPT also stirred up the big tech industry by partnering with the Microsoft's Bing search engine. Google also launched a GPT rival, Gemini, and Baidu introduced its own version called Ernie and Alibaba launched a ChatGPT competitor. These big tech companies are integrating their AI into their product portfolios. Each AI has similar functionality to ChatGPT focused on empowering end-users to complete complex tasks more efficiently.

We're also witnessing the first specialised GPT versions tailored to specific domains. Bloomberg Finance launched Bloomberg GPT, built for finance from scratch, Microsoft introduced BioGPT, an AI model for biomedical data. These specialised AI tools focused on specific knowledge domains and soon, we'll have AI Agent stores where you can buy various types of intelligence, much like Apple and Google's app stores.

The AI arms race has just begun in big tech. It's moving so fast that there will have been a further explosion of innovations before this book even gets to print.

AI's ability to fully comprehend natural language has a profound impact on all our interactions with digital technology. People without any programming or technical expertise can now engage with powerful IT systems. ChatGPT-like natural language technologies have laid the foundations for an entirely new generation of IT applications accessible to a broader audience.

Using these new natural language interfaces, we can all generate high-quality, high-resolution images of virtually anything by simply typing a text prompt, with applications in many different fields. Soon anyone could be an interior designer or architect, only limited by your imagination. Everything you describe can become visible. Applications like ChatGPT, Gemini and Midjourney can generate photorealistic images of people, indistinguishable from real-life photos. This technology can be applied to simple product pictures for restaurants or even entire human models for fashion brands.

The fashion brand Levi Strauss is using AI-generated models to promote and sell their clothes. Consider the implications of this new technology on the photography industry, including models, photographers, studios, stylists, and lighting equipment. This technology allows organisations to conduct marketing campaigns without using a single product. Fashion brand Stradivarius created its first marketing campaign with generative AI, launching an AI-generated campaign for a non-existent AI-generated fashion line. By gauging interest in the fashion items featured in the campaign, they could later produce the fabric and items that people responded positively to, and create them in real life to be sold to a waiting audience. AI enables an entirely different approach to marketing.

If text-to-images isn't enough, consider Sora 2 or Google VEO 3.1 Text-to-Video, which has the potential to replace entire Hollywood film studios and advanced animation studios like Pixar. Simply input a text prompt, and AI generates a high-quality animation or video of a scene in your desired style. This technology is perfect for storytellers and marketers, unlocking a new era and a potential creative revolution.

Hiring a designer to create a landing page, website, or app could soon become obsolete. Google Stich Text-to-UX Design is an AI that designs and creates the user interface for a website or app based on a simple prompt. This AI tool will empower the next generation of web and app developers. What about Text-to-3D Game Design? With tools like Google Genie 3, you can design gorgeous interactive 3D game levels and complex 3D terrains; all based on a single picture as input.

AI lowers barriers and entry levels for many entrepreneurs. Suppose you want to hold a 3D object in your hands, like a prototype of a new product. Text-to-3D Printing allows you to do that without extensive knowledge of 3D printing, accelerating prototyping and product development. Or consider giving textual instructions to a household or factory robot. You can instantly become a programmer of advanced robots without requiring advanced programming knowledge. The potential applications are endless.

Make no mistake: Generative AI is not just another trend, it will be the new interface for everything digital, representing a massive disruptive wave that will transform how we collaborate, imagine, create, and build the world of tomorrow. The best part is that AI adapts to us, allowing us to remain true to ourselves. Ultimately, your own unique qualities will be your selling point in an AI-driven world.

What a wonderful time to be alive.

Chapter 20

AI Generative Engineering and Design

Generative AI is going to have a huge impact on design, engineering, and manufacturing. Our economy is rapidly transitioning away an era of one-size-fits-all mass-produced products, and towards highly personalised ones. Increasingly goods and services will be tailored exclusively to your individual needs where hyper- personalised products will become the norm.

Many of our goods are already created using digital tools such as 3D Computer Aided Design and 3D Computer Aided Manufacture. Powered by the exponential surge in computing power, companies can now conduct advanced virtual simulations with virtual 3D prototypes enabling them to assess a product's performance in the digital world and execute countless iterations in a virtual space. It's now possible to conduct simulated virtual car crashes so real cars don't need to be crashed as often, if at all. This has dramatically cut down on time to market and reduced numerous expensive development cycles.

What if we could supercharge this process by harnessing even greater processing power and the power of AI? The influence of AI on the design and engineering industry is already significant, it's no longer just used for data and sensor information analysis. AI is already revolutionising our entire design and engineering process across almost every industry.

Tools like mid-journey can already design beautiful new products, but mid-journey is merely an AI image generator. It does not understand materials, components, fluid dynamics, or physics. Imagine what could be achieved if AI were to amass this knowledge and bring it all together at an exponential rate. That's exactly what's happening now: AI is learning to generate 3D CAD designs of physical products, understanding how the real world operates and how products and designs function within it. AI is gaining insights into how different materials and constructions respond to external forces and stress. It's a game changing development.

Envision an AI designer with an IQ of 800 that can create products beyond our human imagination. Imagine an intelligent AI system capable of designing and engineering millions of different product versions in seconds and simulating them in a virtual environment based on massive amounts of real-world user data. This is how generative design operates and how many future products will be designed and engineered.

The co-creation of designs created between humans and AI will elevate product design to a whole new level. Products will become exponentially more intricate in structure, yet simpler in operation. The products and the mechanisms to create them will become progressively more sophisticated, lowering the barrier for entrepreneurs to design and create their own products that currently can only be designed and produced by large corporations.

If we look back to the early internet times, only large companies could afford to design and build e-commerce websites. Now, anyone with a smart phone and a good idea anyone can build one in minutes. The same is about to happen with product design and production.

With AI-driven generative design, engineers simply input their design objectives, parameters, and constraints into the design software, and AI takes over. It explores all the potential variations, quickly generating thousands or millions of alternatives. It simulates, tests, and learns from each iteration and applies all the insights it learns during the process. I believe that the result will be products that will start to look more like organic structures, such as bones and muscle formations in our bodies. That's because with AI, we're beginning to design as nature does.

Nature experiments with many versions; if one works, it invests more energy into that design and carries it forward to the next stage. Products will consume fewer materials and, use fewer valuable limited resources, that will be more stress-resistant. As well as designing better products, it's going to massively reduce our resource footprint. A big plus for the planet.

When you merge AI-driven generative design with other groundbreaking technology such as 3D printing, complex and organically shaped structures, previously impossible or costly to produce will see new products becoming both economically viable and physically possible.

So how is the economy going to adapt when AI begins to design even more complex products like cars, houses, and electronic devices? How will our supply and value chains be impacted when AI-designed products can be 3D printed at a hub near you?

There are currently three inter-related, but distinct, disciplines involved getting a product to market; design, engineering, and manufacturing. We are rapidly approaching a point when AI will further unify them and they won't be viewed as separate stages. In an era where customers can design complex products themselves, design, engineering, marketing, sales, service, and support will be fully integrated into one creative and holistic process. The traditional organisational verticals and silos will soon become obsolete.

The era of massive warehouses filled with identical, mass-produced items is nearing an end. We are transitioning to a time of extensive customisation where producing single, bespoke products will be economically viable and when products won't be designed for the average user, but for unique individuals. Your furniture, clothes, smartphone, headphones, and even your toothbrush will be created exclusively for you, fitting your unique needs and preferences perfectly.

Products will evolve from passive and static objects to active, adaptive entities. Products powered by electricity or batteries will soon be equipped with chips, sensors, and broadband; next, they will gain intelligence using AI edge computing chips. Many products will become robotic and autonomous as a result.

A continuous feedback loop from the product's advanced sensors and inbuilt AI connected to the design algorithms will exist, allowing algorithms to learn from the end user's interaction with the product in real life. It will learn from the usage patterns of different target audiences. In other words, products will become intelligent, aware of their environment, and able to constantly adapt. For instance, your smartphone and apps adapt to you and learn from your behaviour. This trend will extend to other products like furniture, cars, and household appliances.

The converging of AI and 3D printing is setting the stage for a future of innovation, customisation, and individuality. The fusion of 3D printing and robotics opens up even more opportunities such as micro-factories. These are autonomous robots combined with 3D printers. The 3D printers produce the parts, and the autonomous AI-powered robots assemble them into a fully functioning finished product. A single micro-factory production line can create a broad range of cheap, fast, and efficient products tailored precisely to consumers' needs.

The future of unique products is on the way and it's custom-made, just for you.

Chapter 21

The Emergence of Large Action Models

Large Action Models are a new frontier in the development of AI. Unlike traditional AI assistants currently confined to answering questions or executing simple commands, Large Action Models are a class of AI models that comprehend natural language instructions and perform complex tasks autonomously.

While AI assistants powered by large language models can predict the next word you are likely to use when you compose a text message, an autonomous agent powered by a LAM can predict the next action in a complex process using language generation, understanding complex reasoning and taking complex actions.

These Large Action Models possess an uncanny ability to grasp our intentions and behaviours, enabling them to operate machine user interfaces and carry out actions for us. Imagine the sheer convenience of simply asking a Large Action Models to book a ride, order online products or services, book a table in a restaurant, or even complete advanced, multi-step business processes - without hassle.

But how do they accomplish such feats? Large Action Models are meticulously trained on extensive datasets of human interaction data, allowing them to learn how to use virtually any app or software, even those without native AI support.

Remarkably, they continuously learn from our feedback and preferences, adapting their capabilities to seamlessly align with our unique needs and habits. These models, also known as Large Agentic

Models or LAMs, combine the language fluency of Large Language Models with the ability to complete tasks and make autonomous decisions, representing a substantial step towards Artificial General Intelligence.

LAMs are meticulously designed to mimic the composition of various applications and human actions, allowing them to operate user interfaces and execute tasks without solely relying on text demonstrations. This capability has been made possible by groundbreaking advancements in neuro-symbolic programming, enabling autonomous agents to comprehend and interpret intricate user interfaces of software systems.

The implications and applications of LAMs are far-reaching. They can automate workflows across all kinds of software systems or leverage simple voice commands to automate complex, multi-step tasks. They can operate a computer's user interface just as a person can, understand buttons and text on websites or in apps, and execute actions based on our voice instructions. We can ask a LAM to operate our computer for us, ushering in a new era of voice-operated operating systems and a wave of screenless devices that will revolutionise how we will interact with computers. Many business applications are currently operated by human beings, requiring extensive training to navigate complex software systems. With LAMs, organisations can build an AI layer on top of their legacy IT systems, enabling users to interact with the AI, which in turn operates the underlying software and fills in the necessary details.

In the realm of cybersecurity and threat detection, financial institutions can implement autonomous agents to continuously monitor network traffic, user activities, and system logs to detect vulnerabilities, and respond to cyber threats in real-time.

While large action models are currently focused on understanding user interfaces on digital devices, this is just the beginning. The true potential unfolds when these models are implemented in robotic devices. Imagine a world where robots, powered by large action models, can operate all the machines and interfaces we have designed for human beings. Robots could operate machines in factories, control

home appliances, navigate electronic devices, and so much more, revolutionising the way we live and work.

As we embrace this technological revolution, it is crucial to consider ethical implications, data privacy, and human oversight to ensure responsible and trustworthy AI deployment. As we stand at the precipice of this exciting frontier, the world of large action models beckons, promising to redefine our interaction with intelligent systems in ways we can scarcely imagine.

Chapter 22

The Rise of Humanoid Robots

Is the rise of the Terminator about to become a reality? As robotics and advanced AI systems converge, how far will that go? In the past, if companies wanted to use robots on production lines or for logistics, they had to buy a robot and hire a team of engineers to program, train, and support it. But things are changing thanks to the self-learning abilities of Artificial Intelligence.

Traditionally, humans had to figure out how to solve automation challenges then translate those solutions into low-level code for robots. It was repetitive and costly, but AI is now flipping the script.

With AI we don't need to crack the problem personally anymore. We present the issue to AI, ask it to solve it, and it develops the code or algorithms to automate the task. Automation is cheaper and more accessible, and by conversing with AI we focus on results - not just processes. Until now, an organisation's success has depended on which brilliant minds they could hire, but AI is turning intelligence into something that's widely available.

Robots and AI are merging in new ways, creating what we call "embodied intelligence." When we think of robots, we think of machines that move. But their real power lies in their AI powered "brain" that provides the rules that guide them. Think of a robot navigating a maze; without AI, it bumps into walls aimlessly, but with AI it can analyse, predict, and decide on the best path, like a smart human decision-maker.

AI gives robots their "brains," but why do they need bodies? AI lives in the virtual world. It can process data, predict trends, and even create music, but to interact with the real world, it needs a body. Enter new age robotics that provides AI with hands, legs, and sensors, a physical form that can touch, feel, and manipulate the world to understand textures, temperatures, and forces bridging the gap between virtual and real.

AI offers intelligence and robotics offer touch and together, they redefine what machines can do. Deep Reinforcement Learning lets them learn from trial and error, adjusting their strategies over time. Transfer Learning allows them to apply skills learned in one scenario to different scenario. Imagine millions of autonomous robots learning and sharing knowledge. These networked autonomous robots will learn a million times faster than an individual robot ever could. This is called Networked Learning. If one robot learns something new, it can be uploaded to an App Store and then all robots with similar form factors can download and use it too. Robot Learning is about dynamic adaptation.

As AI and robotics converge, sensor and perception technology advances rapidly too. AI supercharges robot sensors, enabling them to interpret their surroundings in unprecedented ways. Computer Vision (a subset of AI), enables robots to process visual data, recognise objects, navigate spaces, and differentiate between similar items. Technologies like LiDAR (Laser Imaging Detection and Ranging - or Light Detection and Ranging) and infrared sensors, when combined with AI, give robots a comprehensive view of their environment so they can work in challenging conditions. AI and advanced sensors can already perceive the world almost as intricately as humans can, if not more so.

The line between humans and robots will become ever more blurred. Collaborative robots, or Cobots, are designed to work harmoniously with people, enhancing efficiency and safety. Natural Language Processing (NLP) empowers robots to understand and respond to spoken or written words, making interaction intuitive. Human-robot collaboration is reshaping industries and promising unprecedented possibilities.

With this enhanced mobility and dexterity robots are able to move like us, navigate challenging terrain, and perform precise tasks that were once exclusive to humans. AI driven robotic arms and hands are gaining more precision and finesse every week. In healthcare, robots now assist with precision surgery. Robots offer companionship to the elderly, in agriculture they autonomously plant, water, and harvest crops, enabling more sustainable and cost-effective farming. Manufacturing robots are adapting to assembly line changes and collaborating with humans. Logistics robots are optimised by AI to sort, pack, and deliver packages, navigating complex environments. Meanwhile, research labs are innovating daily, creating robots with tactile sensors that can even mimic human touch. These advancements are reshaping industries, turning what was once fictional into reality that's frightening for many people.

Swarm Robotics

There's another advancement; Swarm Robotics. These are groups of robots networked to each other that work together seamlessly. For example, in agriculture, drones monitor fields and identify issues. In security, robotic swarms offer comprehensive coverage. The potential of swarm robotics continues to expand.

These massive leaps in robot development present us with both ethical and social challenges with concerns about job displacement, safety, and transparency of operations. Although re-skilling and up-skilling can address a certain level of job displacement, some very bright minds are going to be needed to navigate the forthcoming tsunami of change across society. There will be a need for regulations to ensure safety and transparency for AI that will be essential to build trust.

This convergence isn't just a technological marvel, it's a testament to human ingenuity and our quest for progress. As AI provides the intellect and robotics gives it tangible form, technology is redefining the boundaries of what machines can achieve. I urge you to remain curious, stay informed, and engage with progress. The future of AI and robotics is not just in the hands of scientists and engineers, but in the collective consciousness of us all.

Chapter 23

How Far Will AI Go?

To grasp the current AI wave, it's useful to see it within a broader context to understand its relative position compared with prior disruptive waves. That allows you to predict timings and anticipated behaviour in the future. Let's apply the universal principles I have outlined and used them to look at the speed of change.

AI is currently mirroring nature's 6th wave; the intelligence wave. In human terms, it was the 6th wave that enabled humans to learn and adapt in real time. This 6th wave of technology evolution mirrors our adaptation phase, and AI in the cloud empowers people and organisations to learn and adapt in real-time. It's a striking parallel that helps us to foresee the next developments.

Human Brain vs AI Brain

AI is currently undergoing the same developmental stages that a human neocortex goes through in a developing child that we talked about earlier at an accelerated pace. AI already surpasses human capabilities for recognising and interpreting sensor data, comprehending patterns in images and videos, and understanding language through expansive language models.

We are currently entering the exponential phase of the AI S-curve, marked by the rapid evolution of advanced pattern recognition AI systems. Large language models, such as ChatGPT and Google Gemini, exemplify this exponential growth. As AI comprehends natural language, it can process commands in a conversational manner, generating complex texts, images, and videos. This paradigm shift signals technology's adaptation to human needs.

Language with its nuanced contextual variations, poses a significant challenge, but AI is rapidly bridging the gap. Soon, AI will possess a deeper understanding of the external world via sensors and cameras and proficiency in comprehending the conceptual world of language. Consequently, AI systems will be entrusted with increasing responsibilities and decision-making authority.

Following this exponential phase, while AI technology continues to evolve, its societal and organisational impact will begin to plateau. This phase can be likened to the evolution of smartphones, where differences in performance between successive models have become less and less discernible to the average user. With AI, we will witness a comparable scenario. Distinguishing between an AI with an IQ of 800 or 1000 becomes irrelevant, as both surpass human cognitive abilities. Economic pressures to develop even more intelligent AI will wane, as the technology matures.

As AI transitions into truly multimodal systems, it will interface with the physical world through robotics and AI's capabilities will transcend the digital realm, necessitating real-world experiences. Autonomous robots will explore our world much as humans do, grasping the context of our physical world and its understanding of the conceptual world enabling it to make even more nuanced decisions. An essential consideration will be discerning which decisions remain within human purview and which will be delegated to AI.

We are shifting from simple decision-making AI to AI systems entrusted with critical decisions, reshaping every facet of our society.

How Smart Will AI Finally Become?

Let's use the biology example to consider this. Imagine for a moment that there two cells in your body having a conversation discussing how smart the whole neocortex brain is compared to the intelligence of a single cell friend of theirs. They discuss how every tiny cell of your body has a level of intelligence it uses to solve local problems and run the cell day-to-day. The cell is very smart considering how small and apparently simple it is. It can solve many issues on its own and can collaborate with all its neighbouring cells, yet compared to the intelligence of the entire neocortex brain, the intelligence of the cell is insignificant.

In my opinion, the intelligence of AI in the cloud will be of the same magnitude as the intelligence of that one cell compared to the intelligence of an entire neocortex. It will be almost impossible to express that difference in numbers. Even if it was possible, the answer would probably incomprehensible to the human mind.

What about Energy Limitations?

Many people ask me how sustainable AI technology is, with energy consumption so high. I make a comparison with the human body. The human brain uses about 20% of the body's total energy intake; in children, it can be as high as 50%. The brain has all kinds of specialised neural networks, sight, hearing, motor, etc. In the AI space we see a similar processes. Current AI systems are far from efficient. They are trained with inefficient data (current data sources have a high noise to signal ratio) and we use general purpose AI chips which aren't very efficient either.

Our AI systems are early-stage systems and just like the brains of children, they have a lot to learn and therefore consume a lot energy in the early stages of development. So, I expect the power requirements to reduce as the technology matures.

Today, every major AI product (ChatGPT, Claude, Gemini, Sora) is powered by general purpose GPU chips which are not very energy efficient. I believe that within a few years, many large AI models will run on special purpose chips built for that specific purpose. Just like in our brains, where we have brain areas that specialise in processing specific information inputs. That will change everything.

Chapter 24

What Does it Mean for Us?

The speed of development of AI is almost incomprehensible to the human mind, yet it's going to have a deep practical impact on each and every one of us. Many people are already asking how AI will impact our skills and talents and what is it going to mean for our jobs. Let's explore the transformative era of extreme automation, a time when AI is revolutionising our economy and the very essence of our existence.

We are facing a sobering realisation: the hard skills we have honed over centuries are swiftly becoming outdated. Skills that were once fundamental to our economic structure are becoming increasingly automated. Fields such as accounting and law, previously thought to be immune, are now directly in the path of AI's advancing capabilities.

AI's growing prowess in automating complex skills is leading to a significant re- evaluation of tasks that were once held in high esteem. Astonishingly, about 78% of our present job market depends on skills now vulnerable to extreme automation. A revolution where rule-defined tasks are being digitised, automated, and turned into commodities. The flip side is that skills resistant to digitisation are going to gain unprecedented value. Remember, it's not AI alone that poses a threat to jobs, it's the people who adeptly employ AI who will be replacing multiple roles. This evolution challenges us to reevaluate our approach to work, and to redefine value creation in an AI-centric world.

Technological advancement increasingly mirrors our internal world, shedding light on the critical importance of soft skills and intrinsic motivation moving us from focusing on our functional abilities towards a deeper understanding of our inner selves. In an automation-driven world, the absence of purpose and an over-reliance on hard skills could lead to redundancy.

The implications for humanity are immense. As well as job displacement, we are confronting an identity crisis. Our professional identity which, in the past, has been defined by our skill set. We have been educated to almost become robots ourselves to perform hard skills, but AI and robotics are going to outperform us. We are going to be compelled to reconsider the essence of our humanity. The big question is going to be, what will be left?

This transformative era will force us to reevaluate fundamental aspects of our human identity. I envision a world where machines handle routine tasks, allowing people to engage in work that resonates with our hearts. This new epoch is about self-discovery, leveraging technology to forge deeper connections, and emphasising personal growth. In an AI-dominated world our distinct human attributes - our souls - will become our unique value.

Anything that can be digitised will be. In the internet wave we have seen news, music, films and media become commodities. They are cheap and abundant, served via online platforms like X, Facebook, Spotify and Netflix. In the AI wave we will see hard skills go the same way as video tapes, with app stores full of intelligent agents for hire to solve specific problems or perform a hard-skill.

In contrast, we find a spectrum of capabilities that elude digitisation - our soft skills. Traits that are challenging for machines to replicate or automate include empathy, creativity, emotional intelligence, and the ability to connect deeply. Our distinction will no longer lie in executing tasks but in our unique ability to connect, understand, innovate, and inspire.

Preparing for the shift entails a complete transformation of our educational systems, professional development programs, and personal growth strategies. We must transition from traditional training methods to cultivating emotional intelligence and creativity. Those of us who take personal responsibility for doing this for ourselves will be at a distinct advantage. Educational systems haven't yet recognised the future reality of the world our children are going to inherit. Policy makers have a lot of catching up to do. Where they don't, there's going to be disquiet and displacement.

The most important thing to do is nurture the inherent human qualities that lie beyond the reach of the machines. It will aid our survival in an AI-dominated world and will give those that do it the ability to thrive. By embracing our humanity, we can ensure our relevance and enhance our contribution. We have the opportunity to live in a world where humans and machines can coexist in harmony.

AI's impact has the potential to create a more equitable playing field, shifting the focus away from academic achievements and traditional highly valued professions and towards jobs that emphasise our human qualities. AI challenges us to evolve from being human doings, towards becoming human beings once again. It will challenge the ageing perception of what hard work looks like. Currently endurance, long hours and volume of output are badges of honour in many jobs and professions. In the future, hard work will be measured by quality of ideas, imagination and the ability to ask the right questions.

Executives must reconsider their roles. The future CEO may evolve from a Chief Executive Officer to a Chief Ethical Officer, prioritising the ethical and moral implications of AI platforms on all stakeholders. Some jobs will vanish due to full automation, but new, previously unimagined roles will emerge, and they will shape the economy of tomorrow.

As we traverse the transformative landscape of AI, let's keep in mind that while machines take on automatable tasks, they also underscore the significance of our human essence. In the AI-shaped future, it's our soft skills and our human touch that will define our triumphs and our sense of fulfilment.

Part II -
AI's Impact on Society

Chapter 25

Making Sense of Today's Chaos

We are already feeling a massive shift in our society, especially in the West. We are experiencing chaos and struggles as we transition to a new era - and it's not comfortable. We can all feel the wave of change rolling in. People are facing changing employment patterns and a widening of political polarisation, and our freedoms are being reduced on a massive scale. Why is this happening, and what can we do about it? How can we keep our human spark through it all? These are all important questions and the answers can be found in the 7 Evolutionary Waves.

If you put evolutionary waves (including their seven sub-stages) into a matrix, interesting patterns and correlations start to emerge. They tell us what lies ahead in the coming years.

Arthur M. Young demonstrated that halfway through each evolutionary stage, there is a major transformation that becomes a turning point when evolution suddenly makes a U-turn. Young called this The Reflexive Universe. This tipping point doesn't just happen in the big waves, it occurs in each sub-phase too. A tipping point inside each of the mini S-Curves; waves within waves. This theory has been replicated in my own research. It reveals a changing balance between freedom of behaviour, and rigidity of behaviour. A behavioural pendulum swings from one extreme to the other, and back again, through every wave and every S-curve within it.

The phenomenon is visible during our economic and business cycles. When times are good, freedoms are taken for granted. When times get tough, freedoms are reduced, and even fashions change. Some behavioural economists believe they can predict what monetary systems are going to do next by measuring the length of women's skirts and the freedom people have to express themselves. In good times society gets less formal. Dress down Friday's go further and people dress down all the time, even TV journalists present outside broadcasts in open neck shirts with sleeves rolled up. In hard times, dress gets formal again. Ties go back on. People have to go back to the office. Things get more tightly controlled and management enforce rules again. This is a reflection of the freedom/rigidity pendulum, and it affects everything around us.

In changing times rules are needed to give order to the chaos brought about by the rapid technology changes. Once order is restored, the pendulum swings back to freedom again at the end of the wave pattern. That sets up the preconditions for the next wave.

It happens like that in the global economy whenever a new technology brings massive change and opportunity. Fortunes are made, new freedoms and wealth are created - first for entrepreneurs and then for the masses. The unbridled optimism and freedom always gets replaced by the tough reality of implementation and managing the transition period. Financial markets wobble, so controls are brought in, business processes get rigid again, regulators get tougher and political systems start to take over to control of the flow of money. That's the pendulum swinging from freedom to control half way through the wave. Then, once order is restored to businesses, financial systems and markets, ties are loosened again and freedom returns.

Yet again, nature got there first. During the first wave of biological organisms, multicellular organisms floated freely. They were settled in our oceans, gathering food here and there. Their behaviour wasn't conditioned and there was a lot of freedom. If we study the middle of biological evolution and the instinct wave of early reptiles and dinosaurs, you see that they acted completely instinctively and were almost 100% conditioned to dominate and eat. They exhibited very rigid behaviour based on programmed rules and instincts. They had difficulty learning new things and adapting to the changing environment. These organisms had little free will, from an evolutionary perspective. They were at a dead end, and nature realised it was time for a turnaround.

In the latest stage in biological evolution, homo sapiens, free will and behaviours return. This pattern is present in every wave of evolution. If we look at the current state of society, you can see the same rigidity/freedom pattern happening.

Early societies roamed freely and gathered food from their surroundings for a relatively free life. They had virtually no possessions and only owned what they could carry, with few systems or rules conditioning their behaviour. The pendulum was on the side of freedom.

As tribes got bigger, rules and systems were introduced. The pendulum started to swing towards rigidity and freedom decreased. Governments, laws, and regulations took away personal freedoms. In middle of the organisational evolution wave, reptile-like organisations emerged as a result of the need to create calm out of the chaos. Large organisations such as governments, corporates and large NGOs appeared. These organisations act completely instinctively and are almost 100% conditioned. Their rules, procedures, and automation systems hard-wire them for survival, domination, so that they can make profits or measure the effectiveness of their controls. Our current day organisations behave like dinosaurs; hardwired to eat and grow big.

These types of organisations have a tough time learning and adapting to the fast-changing world. They, and the people working inside them, have little free will, and in evolutionarily terms they are at a dead-end. It's time for a turnaround. The pendulum always swings back towards freedom after the rigidity always present in the middle of the S-curve.

It's my view that these technocratic organisations face the same fate as the dinosaurs. Dinosaurs and rules-based organisations that behave like them have the same stage of evolution in common. Both are half way through an evolutionary cycle. This halfway turning point means nothing more than the predicable transformation of an ecosystem.

Dinosaurs dominated the earth for a long time, but progress stagnated and they couldn't adapt to their environment when there was a huge change. In organisational and technological evolution, the same fate is inevitable.

Dinosaur type organisations have dominated the world for a long time, and progress has stagnated. The coming transformation is fierce and radical. But even in a period of turmoil, we can learn from nature that shows how such radical transformations can work.

Consider the transformation from caterpillar to butterfly, one of the most radical transformations observable today. When you understand how nature handles the process, you see how it reflects what is happening in society today.

The economy as we know it can be compared to the caterpillar phase that acts primarily from deficiency needs and a local mindset. If I eat the leaf before you, I have won, and I can grow faster than you. Caterpillars aren't concerned about their environment; they eat everything available. You can't blame them, it's their only purpose; to build a buffer to survive the next stage. Our old economy is like a caterpillar. It's about competition, profit, hard skills, ego systems, a local mindset, and extrinsic motivation.

At the end of their existence in a caterpillar form, the ravenous caterpillar consumes around 200 times its own weight in food, then hangs itself by a thread and turns into a cocoon. They enter the transformation phase holding the buffer of energy from all the food they consumed. They begin a transformation into a new organism; a butterfly. A totally unrecognisable entity from what was there before.

We are in the cocoon phase in our society right now. In nature, the outside of the cocoon hardens to protect what's going on inside it during the transformation. Inside the hard shell, the caterpillar turns into a liquid nutritious soup and that contains all the Imaginal cells holding the blueprint of the butterfly. Bizarrely, the caterpillar's immune system initially attacks those Imaginal cells because, according to the immune system, these weird cells don't belong there. In response, the Imaginal cells start to connect to form larger networks. They develop a critical mass large enough to resist the immune system still present. The networks of cells become more and more powerful. They tune their communications systems and work more closely together, creating resonance and transferring energy. New systems are built that the butterfly is going to need, then something very special happens. There's a trigger moment when a massive crystallisation process starts. A violent moment when the majority of the liquid cells start to resonate with the Imaginal cells. The chaotic soup changes. A completely new internal structure is built quickly, and the butterfly is under construction. The butterfly slowly breaks through the cocoon and the struggle gives the butterfly time to develop enough strength to fly away.

For the cells of a caterpillar to have the potential to transform into a butterfly, they need the right programming. As a cell, you can start fighting against the cocoon, but you must remember that the cocoon offers the protection the cells need to survive during the transformation. Suppose the inner cells destroyed the cocoon during the transformation process; the cocoon's contents would die because it is neither caterpillar or butterfly. It isn't viable without the protective cocoon.

This is precisely the transformation process we are going through in our society right now. We have consumed ourselves in recent decades. We have made our environment almost unliveable. During the COVID 19, we witnessed Governments, NGOs, rules, legislation, and enforcement hardening at a rapid pace and moving towards a totalitarian technocratic system.

We see imaginary cells emerging in our society, people who think and act differently and who want to change the world. These people have a different mindset. They are asking critical and challenging questions. They're viewed as hostile by governments, establishments, and by people who have been indoctrinated by the previous narrative.

Those renegades are censored and suppressed from speaking out, in the same way that the caterpillar's immune system attacks the cells that it doesn't at first recognise. We are seeing an unprecedented attack on free speech happening across societies that previously valued free speech. The inside of our society (individual citizens) is becoming fluid at an accelerating rate. Examples include Brexit, America First, growing individualisation and individual countries starting to hold firm against larger blocks and being punished for being different. Poland, Italy and Hungary are being punished for not toeing the line of EU policy, the bureaucrats are being challenged and their immune system is trying to fight back.

We are witnessing increasing polarisation on social media and more civil unrest. Larger numbers of people are being laid-off, many are becoming self-employed (sometimes voluntarily but sometimes they have no option if they need to work). More people are having to take responsibility for themselves. It's very uncomfortable when the old ways gave the impression of a job for life. Established structures are creaking and slowly losing their value.

Worldwide there are a growing number of networks of differently-minded people who are connecting, inventing and building new structures. They are sustaining communication in online communities. I believe the outside of the cocoon, governments and the established order, will take an increasingly hard line over the next few years. We are heading towards a global technocratic society where the old fabric and societal structures are being deliberately destroyed. Many freedoms will be taken away for us, and people will increasingly resist.

But don't forget that the hardening of the outside (the cocoon) protects the content. If we want butterflies, we should not fight the caterpillar and the cocoon. We need to look for connections in networks and create new systems and structures that make the caterpillar and cocoon obsolete so we can leave them both behind.

"You never change things by fighting the existing reality. To change something, build a new model that makes the existing model obsolete."

Richard Buckminster Fuller

So, What's Next?

We've looked in detail at the drivers behind nature's methods of evolution, now let's take a more detailed look at the driving forces behind technological and organisational evolution. If the ongoing developments are going to serve us, these forces need to relate to human needs.

Whether you put people or cells together in communities, the same type of problems emerge, and are solved with the same kinds of solutions and in the same order. Every major technological change is not only driven by the natural dynamics of the technology problem/solution/problem pattern, it's driven by human needs as well with more than one factor in play.

Back to Maslow's hierarchy of human needs. Although elements of Maslow's research have been supplemented with fresh insight, the key ideas of there being a specific sequence in the way people meet their needs is just as relevant today.

Interestingly, Maslow's hierarchy of needs links perfectly with the Seven Waves. At each level, a new technology helps people manage complexity that's been created as a result of the previous solution. That creates new problems and pain, setting the stage for the next economy. Another new solution emerges, and the cycle repeats itself. In human terms, the solution of each level of problem gives us the time and attention to turn our attention to needs that are one level above in the pyramid. At each level we see that technology fills a need and turns it into a commodity.

- Physiological needs drove the agricultural revolution
- Safety needs drove the industrial revolution
- Love and belongingness needs drove the telecom revolution
- Esteem needs drove the automation revolution
- Cognitive needs drove the social media revolution
- Aesthetic needs drove the AI revolution
- Self Actualisation needs are going to drive the coming holographic revolution
- Transcendence needs will help us transcend into swarm organisations, the first wave of the next seven waves.

At the bottom of the pyramid our basic needs are simply survival; food, safety, sleep, water, warmth, and biological homeostasis. Without these, we die! In the first technological wave, the basic human physiological and biological needs were increasingly met by the technology of the agricultural revolution that delivered stable and larger-scale production and a continuous flow of food. Basic building technology gave us shelter and physical safety. Irrigation technology gave us a continuous supply of water, enabling people to thrive in dry places while fire gave us warmth and light. The first legal systems, laws, and government brought a level of stability, and monetary systems enabled trade and gave us the beginnings of skill specialisation.

The second layer of the pyramid is about the structural avoidance of danger, our security, stability, and comfort. The technological equivalent was the Industrial Revolution that gave us infrastructure technology that stabilised our environment, better building technology that gave us larger towns and cities to house workers who had stable employment. Industrial infrastructure of factories and machinery mechanised tasks. More reliable transportation systems appeared with faster shipping routes, roads, and rail. Technology gave us a constant flow of energy through oil pipelines and, later came cable infrastructure to distribute electricity. Medical technology brought us medicines and healthcare infrastructure providing pharmaceuticals and hospitals helping us in times of illness.

Maslow's third layer of emotional needs, love, connection, belonging and the need for affection had the technology equivalent in the Telecom Revolution. We had systems that connected us over long distances and facilitated communication between loved ones. We could maintain personal and business relationships over long distances with phone systems, fax, radio and television.

Maslow's 4th layer outlines the need for self-sufficiency, status, and being valued by others and technologies 4th layer gave us the automation revolution. Software technology including operating systems appeared, and applications automated all kinds of processes and routines. The software revolution gave technology almost instinctive behaviours that we pre-programmed and made technology easier to use.

The 5th layer of the pyramid outlines our cognitive need for knowledge and meaning. The Internet and the social media revolution met this. Search engines gave us access to knowledge, social networks met our need for self-expression. More recently emerging co-creation communities have appeared that meet our need for purpose and meaning.

The 6th layer of the pyramid is about our aesthetic needs. The AI revolution will provide us with new technologies to help us fulfil these too. Self-learning neural networks will soon create near-perfect algorithms that will improve the beauty and form of products and services. Self-learning systems based on big data will create order and balance in our organisations and ultimately, in our society. Advanced smart virtual agents will help us with all kinds of processes, including self-reflection. Holographic technology will soon be able to build customised education and personal development systems that go beyond anything we can currently imagine. Children will see and feel things visually and be entertained while learning. We won't have to explain everything to students using text. Instead, they'll experience new things through virtual or augmented reality and holographic technology.

The 7th layer of the Maslow pyramid is about our self-actualisation and personal growth needs and the holographic revolution will give us new technologies to meet them. It's likely we will see the arrival of Digital Doubles; virtual versions of ourselves that will act as like intelligent mirror, helping us grow faster. We'll see hive-mind-like technologies and decision-making platforms helping us answer difficult ethical and moral questions collectively, giving us tools that put the needs of many above the needs of self. Co-creation swarm platforms will allow us to holographically collaborate in swarms, giving us meaning and significance and helping us serve our higher purpose and contribution needs.

Technology pushes us higher and higher up the Maslow pyramid. As our needs become easier to manage through technology, we can turn them into cheap and easily available commodities and start focusing on our next level of needs. As we stack systems on top of each other, technology pushes us more and more to the top of the pyramid.

Interconnectedness Is Coming

Imagine a world where humanity takes its next evolutionary step. Instead of isolated individuals striving for personal success, we move to an interconnected whole, united by a shared purpose. Just as the 7th layer of self-actualisation invites us to realise our full potential, the transcendence layer challenges us to go beyond ourselves, merging our individual aspirations with the collective good.

Just as cells come together to form the intricate symphony of a human body, each of us has a unique role to play in creating a thriving planetary organism. What would it mean for you if your talents and passions could ripple outward, contributing to a greater consciousness that uplifts everyone? Emerging technologies like AI and collaborative platforms aren't just tools, they are bridges enabling us to connect, co-create, and evolve together.

The good news is that transcendence doesn't erase individuality; it amplifies it. It allows each of us to shine brighter as part of a unified whole. You can embrace this shift by cultivating a mindset of collaboration, exploring the potential of technology, and finding purpose in contributing to something far greater than yourself. Together, we can unlock a future where humanity thrives not in isolation, but in harmony, as a collective consciousness shaping a better world.

Each technological revolution allows us to better meet our latent needs. Technology helps us manage complexity and focus on our higher requirements, pushing us towards the top of the Maslow pyramid.

Many in parts of the Western world have arrived at the top part of the pyramid already. But most people and organisations still have a mindset rooted in the bottom layers, so there is still work to do and the technology of the 6th and 7th waves will help us with that.

Above the seven needs, there is an eighth layer; our transcendence needs. Our need to merge into the greater whole, to be at one as a larger organism. In my view, this is the first wave of the next 7 wave cycle.

To thrive in the 6th, 7th, and 8th layers of Maslow's hierarchy we must embrace a blend of skills and mindsets that elevate not just ourselves, but the world around us. We start with aesthetic thinking and creativity; the ability to see beauty in the everyday and express it through art, design, and how you solve problems. Paired with self-awareness and authenticity, this allows you to align your actions with your true values, fostering your personal growth and fulfilment. As you move toward transcendence, you cultivate empathy and compassion and open your heart to the needs of others and find purpose in contributing.

This might sound a long way off, but the tools to achieve these states are already within your reach. Practicing mindfulness and reflection keeps you present and connected, and nurtures your openness to expanded perspectives. There are already apps for that!

Engaging in activities that bring you joy and meaning, whether creating, collaborating, or simply appreciating the world's beauty can be done with or without technology. Every small step you take, a moment of gratitude, a kind gesture, or a creative spark, ripples outwards and shapes a future where humanity can thrive together. The journey to transcendence begins with a single step, and the possibilities are as limitless as your imagination.

Some people will start to wonder what the human role is in this evolutionary process. Will we soon be made redundant by robots and AI? Personally, I don't think so. Biological systems such as our neocortex brains haven't made individual cells in our bodies obsolete because without cells, there is no body and without a body, there is no brain. Every tiny cell is a building blocks of the society we call our bodies. And now we humans have also become building blocks in the society of humanity.

Systems like AI are just a facilitator to connect people, empower them and increase our survival chances. In biology, all biological systems in our bodies aim to empower the individual cells in our bodies and allow each cell to focus on their purpose. Our technological systems will do precisely the same for us.

"We can't solve problems by using the same kind of thinking we used when we created them".
Albert Einstein

Each new wave forces us to raise our awareness and consciousness forcing us to adopt a new perspective and grow our mindset and adapt to new situations. That's why we need to adopt a future-proof mindset, only then can we solve the problems we have created in decades past.

Chapter 26

The Human Legacy

Dealing with Disruption

Although we have the power to focus on higher growth needs, most of us are still stuck in a deficiency needs mindset asking ourselves if we have enough money to pay the bills, if our bonus is big enough this year or if we have enough land or property to secure our future. Life is still about competition.

To progress as a society, we will need to let go of that and move more toward the next layer of needs. Transformation is going to happen, whether we like it or not. Although that sounds scary, there are possibilities that lie on the other side.

No transformations happen without a solid ecosystem. Our modern technology exists because of layers of ecosystems stacked one on top of the other. Stacking ecosystems is a mirror of what nature has done and we have enough ecosystems stacked up to allow us to transform society.

Technology is allowing us to gain more control over our destiny. The way we earn money is moving away from being reliant on a corporate entity towards using platforms that allow us to be part of a bigger self organising system allowing us to work independently. Companies like Grab (35 million customers and 13 million drivers and merchants in South East Asia) have no physical cabs on the balance sheet.

These kinds of companies leverage underlying existing ecosystems. When you zoom into the Interaction layer, there are millions of people who simply want to get from A to B, and cab drivers who want to get them there. There's lot of legislation for taxis, but on the ground, you see people taking control of their own livelihoods and transport needs. A friend who recently visited Thailand told me how the licensed taxi ranks had lines of empty cabs while Grab drivers were banned from using ranks to pick up passengers, but people were making their own choices. Grab customers walked a few metres, used the app to hail a ride and were on their way. You just bid for a ride, choose your size and level of luxury, accept a fare you're happy with, the money goes straight off your card and you can leave a tip for good service through the app at the end of the ride. You rate your driver (an incentive for drivers to be nice!) and there's a safety button if you feel worried during the ride. Licensed taxis in Asia are notorious for turning off the meter and there's no safety net. So, customers and drivers have used technology to get around complex bureaucracy, improve safety, and get better service. Asians are taking transport into their own hands without interference from above.

None of this could have happened without the technology layers underneath. There's the infrastructure layer of the roads, energy and cars (and with Grab, tuk-tuks or mopeds). There are the GPS sensors at the Information layer that transmit driver and the customer location, wireless data networks and information processing contained in cloud servers and our smartphones. At the Automation layer, there are phones with apps, app stores, and operating systems. There's an extensive automation network already in place to build on.

The social media wave that represents the cognitive wave gives us online communities, big data and analytic tools. Companies like Grab sit on top of all of that, creating an interface that activate all ecosystems at once. Disruptive companies do this really well, building an interface that leverages existing ecosystems to their advantage. That's how these companies grow so fast and have such a huge impact. Grab co-founder Anthony Tan said "Providing 13 million gig jobs is probably the largest impact and poverty alleviation on a grand scale and it's working in 750 cities. Our calling is really clear, how do we make sure no one is left behind?"

The company was only founded in 2012. By 2018 it became so successful it took over Uber's assets in the region. Growth at this scale is only possible thanks to apps, smartphones and massive computing power. These layered ecosystems mean you don't have to worry much about your lower-level needs anymore. They give you space to focus on your higher needs. We're going to switch from ego systems, the competition based individual mindset, towards more ecosystems based on relationships and collaboration. These systems can facilitate a reduced dependence on governments, doctors, teachers, or your boss - and give you the opportunity for greater independence.

Make no mistake, the system is fighting against this transfer of power from the few to the many. Witness the attacks on free speech, the increase in regulation and the intrusive oversight of our social media activity and communications, the control of mass media, the push to dispense with cash and the snoop on how we spend our money. These are all symptoms of dinosaur systems attempting to survive.

But we have our own minds. We can decide what we choose to accept.

Increasingly it's possible to generate an income independently and participate in the bigger system without someone else controlling us. We don't have to depend on one company or person for our future security anymore. These ecosystems work as a buffer to take us to the next stage.

Think of the caterpillar eating itself to create a brand-new ecosystem that can serve as a cocoon in a transition period to get to the point where the butterfly emerges. There is an obvious purpose for the cocoon. Even if it's uncomfortable and seemingly hopeless at first, the cocoon protects the content for the next phase. The ecosystem protects the butterfly while it makes its transformation. With new technologies we are creating a new interface every time that allows us to manage the complexity of the underlying layer effortlessly. We are seeing one ecosystem after another evolve, giving us an ever-increasing stack of ecosystems at our disposal.

We will soon be moving more to an economy where we have products as a service. When you need a product, it will be there for you, and when you no longer need it, you'll be able to stop your subscription or recycle it back to your 3D printer, ready to create the next thing.

There will be infrastructure as a service too; the Internet of things. Infrastructure where you can place a package somewhere that will automatically arrive at its destination. It already happens with virtual packages via the internet. You can already download a program that contains the specification for an item so you can print the product yourself on your 3D printer.

We will soon have information as a service. Abundant data of 4G and 5G networks are already here, so on-demand data will be available anywhere anytime. Broadband data is already a commodity, like water from the tap. We've seen the rise of software as a service in recent years. You don't have to buy an expensive software license anymore, you just use a system from the cloud for a relatively low monthly fee. When you don't need it anymore, you cancel.

There's been a huge expansion of platforms as a service. Amazon and Ebay are great examples. Amazon can take care of your whole business with a web-shop, logistics, payment system and everything behind your storefront. They even hold the inventory so you don't have to hold stock. Millions of small businesses have been built on this ecosystem. Platforms even allow you to build your own smartphone app for a few dollars a month. These are mature technologies already.

In the 6th sixth wave, the AI wave, you will be able to get intelligence as a service. If you have a problem you want to solve or a service you want to develop, you can throw as much intelligence at it as you want for a low monthly fee. When you don't need it anymore, you just stop it and stop the cost.

I believe we're going to get more and more things as a service because of these stacked ecosystems. Small startups will increasingly leverage all them to create compelling services and products. AI, algorithms, and robotics will automate the bottom of the pyramid in the same way that the internal processes in our biological systems are fully automated. You don't have to worry about your blood flow, your heart pumping, or your digestive system starting in the morning. It happens automatically. The internal processes in our society, like food and infrastructure will soon be almost completely automated and we will start focusing on the top of the Maslow pyramid. Machines will primarily fulfil most of our everyday needs and people will start focusing mainly on the who, the why, and on their soft skills.

That's where our role as humans will increasingly go in the future. Technology will soon be doing all the hard skill stuff. But people still have to think about why we're doing things, and who is the right person to get it done.

"If I've seen further than others, it is by standing upon the shoulders of Giants.'

Isaac Newton

Every new technology wave that builds on the previous wave has us standing on the shoulders of giants. We've already seen that in biological evolution and with all the evolutionary waves that came before us. We can do great things as humans thanks to the many enabling ecosystems we already have.

Part III

Chapter 27

AI's Impact on Organisations

From Competition to Collaboration

Let's take a look at AI's impact on our organisations. What will they look like in the future? What structures will they have, and how can they be future-proofed?

Halfway through the seven evolutionary waves there is always a turning point. In the biological waves the turning point occurred in the reptilian brain of dinosaurs. The first waves were about competition but the later waves were about cooperation. Dinosaurs weren't good at working together, mammals got better and apes better still. Humans excel at cooperation.

Today the same things are happening in organisational terms. Small communities of entrepreneurs are going through the seven stages of evolution and building newer organisations faster than ever before. Grab is less than 20 years old. Coca-Cola took 80 years to build a comparable infrastructure.

These new organisations are more adaptable to their environment and cheaper to build. Funding an internet start-up around 2002 cost around $5M. Funding one in 2014 cost around 5K; a 99.89% cost reduction. Today you can start for less than a few hundred dollars. If you work quickly enough you can get started for free using trial periods on tech platforms and only pay when you scale up.

We are witnessing a divide in the seven waves, the big reset halfway through the process. We still have a generation of old dinosaur-like organisations with DNA that inclines them to think that by sharing their knowledge, they lose their competitive advantage.

I believe that the next generation of organisations will have more primate like-like characteristics. They'll be much better at cooperating. Eventually in wave 7 organisations will exhibit much more human-like social empathetic characteristics and get really good at working together at a massive scale.

We can see seeds germinating already with tie-ups between brands, product placement in films and on TV where companies like Disney and food businesses who share target customers leverage each other's brands for mutual gain.

Google and META (formally Facebook) are also trying different new ways of working. Google's holding company Alphabet is more than just Google. It's a huge group of small start-ups working together inside one larger colossus, a larger herd. Although these tech companies are massive, they aren't dinosaurs. They are younger and have their roots in a disruptive mindset. They envisioned things that others couldn't, long before they became a reality and though established names today, when they started, they were highly disruptive. Though they aren't immune from evolution. As they grew bigger, they needed to create order from rapid growth, so layers of management tried to suppress competition. Although they are more mammal-like, they haven't totally let go of some dinosaur elements. Old DNA can creep back in.

Things are changing so rapidly that collaboration is going to be the only survival option left. Organisations that can't, or won't cooperate, will die.

We are currently at the halfway stage of the S-Curve where a reset happens when it feels like chaos (and it is) because so many changes are happening simultaneously. Developments are exponential with an exponential number of connections are being made, hence the chaos. Yet it is from that, that completely new structures emerge.

How To Become A Future-Proof Organisation

Changes due to AI are speeding up change so quickly, how can you create something you can't visualise? What will organisational culture look like? What will a future proof organisation need from its employees?

Man-made organisations evolve in several phases. Each phase brings a new type of organisation with new skills and properties based on new technological systems. During each technological wave communication technology emerges that allows people to manage the complexity of large-scale communication. What most people underestimate is how complex that is and how much that complexity increases during each phase.

10x Complexity

Complexity of organisations increases approximately tenfold after each new technological wave. In other words, each new technology wave or interface simplifies managing complexity tenfold, leading to increased technological empowerment with each wave. Consequently, each technology wave makes it 10x easier to organise ourselves and at the same time we need to use 10x less energy to get the improvement. Therefore, in the next decade, we can expect to witness a 10x10 = 100-fold increase in the efficiency of organisations. With AI combined with holographic technology, we can organise ourselves extremely efficiently.

Because the most complex part of an organisation is communication (between departments, individuals, customers, and the outside world), communication becomes ever more complex the bigger the organisation grows.

To give you a quick picture of that, I've illustrated the communication technologies that have emerged in each wave, relative to the business structures and business complexity. On the left , a column contains the communication technologies present in each of the seven waves. In the middle column, we there's the organisational structures; their physical structures. On the right, there's a number showing complexity of that organisation; that complexity is the number of people who can work together simultaneously. The more people who work together simultaneously, the greater the complexity becomes because you have to coordinate and manage it all in real-time.

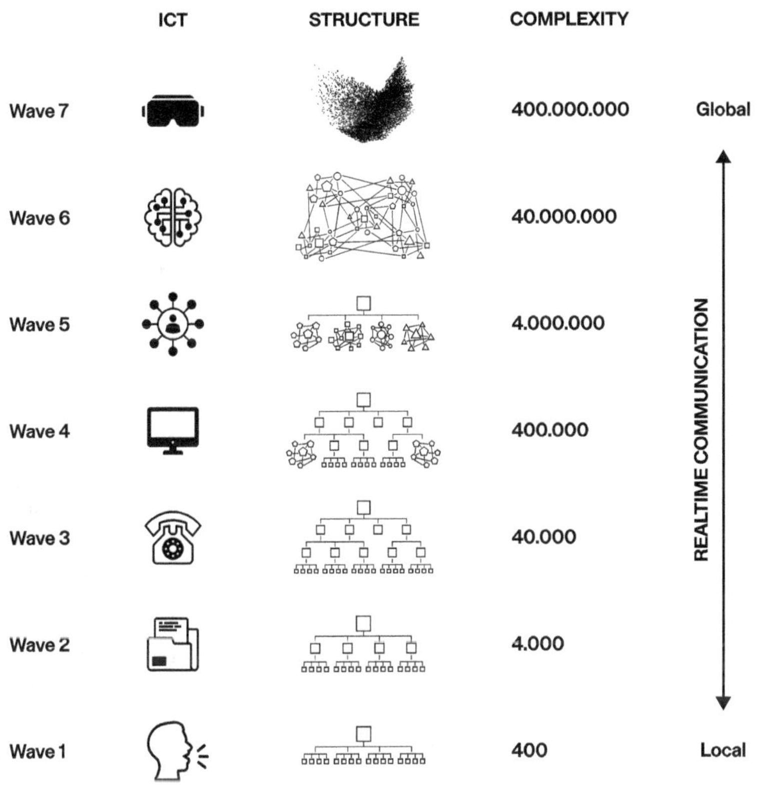

The agricultural revolution saw the first emergence of small local organisations. The first settlements were very flat organisations of just a few hundred people. Even then, there were a lot of things to manage; justice had to be done and rituals to be followed. Despite the small numbers, it was still difficult.

The Industrial Revolution wave that followed saw a tenfold increase in complexity as organisations grew to thousands of people. Henry Ford had around 3,500 people working simultaneously in his US factories. He managed by creating sub-departments that had their own sub-tasks. There was one chief, Ford, and below him managers who each led a separate department. With the help blueprints, processes, procedures, and guidance documents Ford could distribute the work. Parts were made separately and assembled centrally. A complete Model

T-Ford rolled off the assembly line at the end of the process. So, in the 2nd wave there was a top management layer, sub-management layer underneath, and finally the factory workers.

In the 3rd wave, the Telecom Revolution, the management pyramid got more hierarchical as the organisational size grew. AT&T had tens of thousands of people working simultaneously. That was only possible because of better telecoms; better voice lines, telex, telegraph, and fax enabling them to grow from a local to a national organisation. Employees could stay connected over long distances, but that added another layer of management with multiple geographic branches; HQ for top management, geographic branch managers, below them another layer of management, and the local employees.

In the 4th Automation wave, there's was another tenfold increase in organisational complexity. IBM had hundreds of thousands of people working simultaneously. IBM was a global firm, enabled by tools that facilitated the automation of internal business processes; digital transaction systems, enterprise systems like ERP and CRM, and computers in different departments linked together. They could communicate with each other and transactional information like orders and deliveries were shared more efficiently. This extra functionality had a hierarchical structure that gained more layers, and more complexity.

This is how organisations become hierarchical and bureaucratic. The organisational structure itself has become a system of its own that's hard-wired to enforce specific behaviours, and it starts to build its own immune system to ensure its own survival.

In the 5th Internet and Social Media wave, the tenfold increase happened again. Companies like Uber and Grab have millions of drivers working together with the efficiency of a swarm. Corporate structure is becoming flatter. There's still headquarters with a CEO, a Board of Directors and management, but underneath there are smaller swarms. There are countries with their own regulations, each with swarms of drivers working together as one collective. This is possible because of the ecosystems including App Stores, fast wireless internet, and all kinds of online tools.

In the next AI wave, organisations comprising tens of millions of individuals will be able to collaborate seamlessly, forming an even more fluid swarm. AI is great for managing complexity and enabling large groups to work together in harmony. New organisational structures will become more fluid, increasingly moving towards swarm-like organisational structures. In swarms it's challenging to define the management layers because the leadership is not hierarchical; it becomes situational. Leadership depends on the situation in which the organisation finds itself in any given moment.

The 7th wave of holographic technology will enable completely new forms of co-creation. New organisational structures will make collaboration possible on a global scale. When we can holographically connect with each other in real-time over vast distances, without language barriers, regardless of time and location, we will likely to be able to establish organisations comprising hundreds of millions of individuals who can collaborate seamlessly as a unified entity.

Organisations have gone from a local level to a global level because of ever newer communication interfaces and real-time technologies that keep us connected and in communication over longer distances. The more real-time those communication tools become, the more fluidly organisations will move, and in turn the ever more fluid they will become.

The Magic of the Swarm

At this point it's worth observing how swarms work in nature. In small groups of animals, you tend to see a leader. Lions have a pride leader, herds of horses have a lead mare, but when the number of participants get to roughly over 50, you don't see hierarchical structures anymore. At this point nature switches to another phenomenon; swarms. We see this swarming behaviour in birds, insects, fish and herds of mammals. An important characteristic of natural organisational forms is that everything moves effortlessly. There is a flow that needs no management to structure things.

Flocks of birds, for example, move as one fluid super-organism. Research at Stanford University discovered that each bird keeps an eye on the six or seven birds closest to it. Each bird constantly calibrates their actions with those seven others. If one bird moves aside, the rest move with it. They all keep an eye on each other and maintain certain basic rules, 1) fly in the same direction as your neighbour, 2) fly at the same speed as your neighbour 3) don't collide with other birds.

When birds in a flock follow these three rules, the first basic swarm characteristics begin to emerge. Of course, many more rules apply, but this goes beyond the scope of this book. If people followed such simple rules, we could make big steps at an organisational level. You probably have already witnessed that the simplest rules seem challenging to follow within organisations. That's because we are still working on an old paradigm. People are working to rules set by others they can't see and don't interact with. Layers of management and complexity get in the way, the more rules the more static and organisation becomes.

We need to move to a different form of communication where we continuously monitor the people and other entities around us. If we can start doing that, we will have organisations that work like a fluid swarm of individuals working together as one big organism, adapting to the changing environment in real-time, all the time.

When dangers come from the environment swarms react immediately. Future organisations need to speed up so they can do the same. There are no CEO birds, Board of Directors' birds or management birds flying above the swarm, directing the whole to go left or right. They are autonomous, self-aware organisations where each individual has a key part to play.

From a social perspective, connecting with others also serves as a mechanism to absorb tensions. When a bird of prey approaches a flock it charges shape, yet still it remains as one entity. The Max Planck Institute discovered that swarms are significantly more effective and efficient solving problems or preventing dangerous situations. They are extremely agile by nature, and continuously adapt with almost no effort. We need that kind of wisdom and smart behaviour if our organisations are going to survive the rapid changes ahead. These organisations are wise because AI can soon utilise the collective knowledge and experience of all their members (employees) to make wise decisions.

The 6th and 7th waves of technology will make that wisdom possible.

Granular details about the potential of swarm organisations are beyond the scope here, but to learn more check out Evert Bleijenberg's book "Swarm Organisations". Evert and I are working together to develop a platform so swarm inspired behaviour can become a reality for organisations and communities. There is a technology-based solution just around the corner. We believe that swarm organisations are more future-proof than any traditional ones. They're more resilient, adaptable, robust, efficient, and more rewarding to work in.

Real Time Adaptive Ability

Solid pyramid-like organisational structures aren't very adaptable, but fluid organisations are. They are also more innovative because people tend to place themselves where their skills are best used and are more valued for their contribution.

Nature has been organising itself for billions of years, so it offers valuable lessons for us once again. Cells exhibit natural behaviour. When relaxed, the cell walls facilitate the transport of information and resources, allowing for more efficient flow in and out of the cell. The cells is more creative, innovative and can solve problems. And so it is with people.

Swarm organisations continuously adapt to stay relevant in their surrounding ecosystem instead of cumbersome clusters that ramble on in the same old way. They are living systems that adapt to their environment.

Ultimately, I predict that organisations will evolve into something more akin to an orchestra where each individual inside will play the instrument best suited to them. The conductor will be an AI algorithm that makes sure the right people do their job at the right time and contribute with a passion to the larger, harmonic whole. Together, they produce a symphony.

Leadership will be less about the psychology of how to pressure and push people to show certain behaviours and more about ecology: so how to generate, create, and facilitate an ecosystem where everyone can do their own thing and be supported by everyone else, for the benefit of all. The big challenge for leaders is going to be how they can create a culture where there is harmony and synergy.

Connecting is the Key

Stanford University did a 25 year study to uncover the qualities of the most successful and resilient organisations. Surprisingly, the ones that stood out were not the organisations with the latest technology or the newest business processes, they were the ones with high levels of emotional intelligence where people stayed connected to each other, even in difficult times. They created breakthroughs - where other companies were more likely to have breakdowns.

Emotional intelligence will play a significant role in the future, and swarm technologies will facilitate real emotional connections between people. We are going to need to excel at connecting. The better people get at that, the better they function as a swarm.

With every biological upgrade we've seen in organisms, a different kind of consciousness has emerged. Early organisms were reactive, following next generations became more adaptive and reacted better to their environment. When nervous systems evolved and sensors became effective, organisms developed an attentional consciousness. They could focus on things outside themselves and started to show new behaviours, like hunting.

The reptilian brain created an executive-like consciousness, where organisms showed more executive behaviours. The limbic brain gave organisms emotional awareness, and they became more aware of other organisms, emotions, and feelings. The neocortex brain brought self-awareness, and organisms became aware of who or what they were, and more aware of their social environment. The 7th biological wave brought social and empathic awareness. Organisms started to exhibit increased empathetic social behaviour.

Today's new wave of technologies brings us to the level of AI in the cloud. Organisations that harness AI to process vast amounts of information are going to become increasingly aware of their own behaviour and environment in real-time leading to swarm behaviours. To reach this level of awareness, traditional organisations will need to take radical steps.

Mindset Levels

Let's translate the seven levels of consciousness/awareness into some basic mindset levels using a well-known four-level mindset evolution model (often used in human-centred innovation, conscious leadership, and organisational transformation contexts). These concepts are observable human behaviours.

The model contains four main mindset levels. At the bottom is the victim mindset. Sadly, a large proportion of the world's population reside here. With a victim mindset, when something goes wrong the fault or blame is put onto someone or something external; a director, manager, doctor, prime minister, situation, or even a God. Victims rarely look inside themselves for causality. It's most prevalent when people are dependent on a system; an organisation, director, doctor, government, or a religion. People are motivated extrinsically, working for money as their external incentive.

Next up is a Responsible mindset, the first step towards personal freedom. You see it when people recognise a problem and show ownership and accountability. Therefore, they gather together some community members or colleagues and decide to solve it themselves. People with this mindset show more ownership and responsibility.

Next level up again is an entrepreneurial mindset that's much more creative. These people have entrepreneurial drive. They see opportunities everywhere and feel they have the power to make cool new things, make the world a better place and benefit themselves and others. People here are intrinsically motivated.

At the top level, there's a purpose-driven mindset of joy and passionate involvement. People here are highly intrinsically motivated by their passion or purpose. They don't work for money; they work for a higher cause.

Victims vs Positive Action

All companies would like their employees to have a purpose-driven mindset, but most are still in a victim mode, creating a fragmented organisational culture. This is where fear drives behaviours; fear of making mistakes, losing a job or being overtaken or overlooked. People focus on their own deficiency needs and when that's the driving force, they are defensive towards other people or groups. Cultures are closed. People and departments keep things to themselves worrying if they share, someone else will run with their ideas and they lose personal advantage, and their personal value is diminished.

The next generation of organisations will need to evolve towards a cultural synergy more akin to swarms, with an open culture where people proactively do things themselves for the good of the whole and where creativity is king.

For traditional organisations to survive they will need to bridge this chasm. They will need to create an environment of psychological and emotional safety. That's challenging in a centralised hierarchical organisation. The challenge ahead is to create an environment where people bring their whole being to work, their ups and downs, without fear of being judged, where they don't have to be afraid for their job or promotion if they do something different. When the bridge is there, it's possible to create a culture where people can relax, and as you know from our study of nature, when each cell (person) in a body (organisation) is relaxed, the walls are thin and flexible, information can get through and communication gets easier.

The Culture of Swarms

When you build a bridge to safety, people get more creative and innovative, mistakes are allowed, and even promoted as positive learnings. Elon Musk said "Failure is an option here. If things are not failing, you are not innovating enough." His companies are known for being innovative, fast growing and pivoting as needed. Like him or hate him, he's got a track record of building high growth businesses with a workforce that shares his passion and purpose.

The more mistakes you make, the more you learn. If more organisations create this kind of environment, there'll be a massive change in culture, mindset, and behaviour. Research backs this up. Google has researched how to develop a more agile and adaptive culture. They commissioned a study across hundreds of teams worldwide. They found that emotional and psychological safety came out top. With security people dare to be vulnerable and air ideas that may seem very crazy at first, but lead to new insights and eventually to breakthroughs.

Daring to be vulnerable in your professional environment is something that isn't possible in many organisations today. But as more leaders focus on it becoming a cultural norm, there will be more breakthroughs and larger numbers of future proof organisations. There's no doubt that it's difficult, especially in large dinosaur-like organisations, and for many it may not be possible. Most dinosaurs couldn't adapt their DNA in time to survive. Though birds, direct dinosaur descendants, did survive. Their small size and ability to work in groups was key to their survival and ongoing evolution. When it comes to companies, some dinosaurs may shift, though many will struggle to adapt and go the same way that T-Rex did. The adaptable ones will fly high.

"Swarms exist by the moral contract that all will participate and benefit equally and proportionally while keeping their sovereignty."

Evert Bleijenberg

For a swarm to work, it's important for everyone within it fully participates and maintains their individuality. Maybe there's hope for us if we can do that. If we can, we can make a massive impact, independent of technology and in the face of the threats around us. If we can grow this mindset and develop the technology to make it to work, we can build future-proof organisations and a better future of us all.

Chapter 28

The Future of Work in the Age of AI

What it would be like if organisations stopped enforcing rigid hierarchies and top-down decision-making? What if they functioned more like flocks of birds or schools of fish; moving fluidly, adapting instantly, and thriving in the face of uncertainty?

Swarm organisations are a revolutionary model inspired by nature and powered by AI. I believe they represent the future of work, reshaping how we think about leadership, collaboration, and innovation. How can we adapt and thrive in this new paradigm?

The AI-Powered Nature of Swarm Organisations

Decentralised, self-organising systems mimic the collective intelligence of natural swarms such as bees, ants, or birds. With no single leader dictating every move, individuals work autonomously and align with a shared purpose. The group adapts quickly to changes, solves complex problems, and continuously innovates. A murmuration of starlings has thousands of birds moving in perfect harmony, responding to each other and their environment in real-time. Swarm organisations operate in much the same way, using AI and digital tools for seamless communication, coordination, and decision-making across teams.

AI is at the heart of these organisational swarms. It is the connective tissue that enables real-time data sharing, decision-making, and coordination. Here's how:

1. **Real-Time Communication:** Just as birds in a flock share information instantly, AI-powered platforms allow team members to communicate and collaborate in real time, no matter where they are.

2. **Distributed Decision-Making:** AI tools analyse vast amounts of data providing insights and recommendations, empowering individuals to make informed decisions without waiting for approval from above.

3. **Dynamic Role Assignment:** Roles are fluid. AI can identify who is best suited for a task based on skills, availability, and the needs of the moment. Resources are used efficiently.

4. **Swarm Intelligence:** By aggregating the knowledge and input of all members, AI enables the organisation to act as a single, intelligent entity--adapting to challenges in ways that no individual could achieve alone.

The Human Side

While AI is a powerful enabler, swarm organisations are ultimately about people, requiring a fundamental shift in how we think, work, and lead. The new demands will be:

1. **Behavioural flexibility and Continuous Learning** - Change is constant. Roles, tasks, and priorities can shift in an instant, and individuals must be ready to pivot. This means embracing continuous learning and openness to new ideas, technologies, and ways of working.

2. **Collaboration and Emotional Intelligence** - Collaboration is key. Success depends on your ability to work effectively with others, build trust, and navigate diverse perspectives. Emotional intelligence; understanding and managing your own emotions while empathising is essential.

3. **Autonomy and Self-Responsibility** - Without a traditional hierarchy, individuals must take greater responsibility for their actions and contributions, needing self-motivation, discipline, and a strong sense of purpose.

4. **Technological Proficiency** - As AI becomes integral, technological proficiency is no longer optional. You'll need to understand how to use digital tools and platforms to enhance your work and collaborate effectively.

Speed Matters

Swarms aren't just a trend, they're a response to growing complexities and uncertainties. Traditional hierarchies with their rigid structures and slow decision-making are ill-suited to the challenges of the 4th Industrial Revolution. By contrast, swarm organisations are designed to thrive on change and capable of adapting to new opportunities and challenges in real time leveraging the collective intelligence of members. They are highly resilient and built to withstand disruptions and grow stronger from them.

"Imagine a world where uncertainty is not a barrier but a bridge to something greater. What would it mean for you to cross that bridge?"

Christian Kromme

How To Thrive

Don't have to wait for your organisation to adopt swarm principles, begin today:

1. Embrace Change and start viewing it an opportunity rather than a threat. Practice stepping out of your comfort zone and trying new approaches.
2. Invest in Learning by dedicating time to develop skills essential in swarm organisations; adaptability, collaboration, and technological proficiency.

3. Foster Collaboration by building strong relationships with colleagues and look for ways to contribute to collective success for your team.
4. Leverage Technology by experimenting with AI tools and platforms to enhance your productivity and decision-making.

Swarm organisations offer an incredible opportunity: the chance to thrive in a world of constant change. The question is, are you ready to embrace them? By developing the skills and mindset needed to succeed inside them, you can position yourself not just to survive, but to lead in the age of AI.

> **"The future belongs to those who can adapt, collaborate, and thrive on uncertainty. What role will you play in shaping it?"**

Chapter 29

How Will Your Company Evolve?

How can traditional organisations transform into more fluid structures to survive and grow? What challenges will they face?

It's evolutionarily logical for organisations to evolve their structure to become more swarm-like. Cooperating on a large scale is the only solution to survive. Less competition and more collaboration will be essential.

You've read a lot about S-Curves already, because they are a key part of evolution, and organisations are no exception. In every situation, the first part of that S-Curve is about competition, every man (cell/plant/organism/organisation) for himself, and the second part is about collaboration and cooperation where all have to form one greater whole. And remember there's a tipping point halfway through each curve.

When atoms worked together, they built molecules, and when molecules worked together, they built cells. When cells worked together, they built massive organisms. Now that people can work together, we can build bigger, more complex organisations. For our evolutionary S-Curve to follow its natural progression it's essential we start working well together.

The technologies we need to collaborate on a global scale are already here, and they're getting better every day. We now need to start developing the mindset to take full advantage of the benefits on offer.

Dinosaur-like organisations rigid with little freedom of movement. Swarms are free structures based on fluid mechanics, able to move in any direction in a heartbeat. As far as we know, it is virtually impossible to modify a living organism's DNA to create another organism. What organisms can do is to create offspring able to adapt to the environment better than their parents did.

Our children are growing up with all sorts of new technologies that they consider normal, but for the majority of parents it's all still slightly scary, and so it has been for millennia. The few successful offspring of dinosaur-like animals were more mammal and bird like. Birds, the most highly successful dinosaur descendants, still thrive today. The same is true for large organisations. It's challenging for them to adjust their DNA; the internal culture.

Consider the Grab co-founder Anthony Tan. His father was President of a large company that assembles Nissan cars in Malaysia. His grandfather pioneered the Japanese automotive industry in Malaysia. They knew about cars but weren't interested in his idea for an app. It was probably too far out of their comfort zone or level of understanding to support. But Tan understood the transport market and educated himself on new technology. That next generation of new ideas built on top of old problems and created a new opportunity.

Even with powerful and visionary leaders at the top, you're going to struggle to modify the organisational culture by force. So, what larger organisations can do instead, is to create as many 'offspring' as possible.

Not everyone has a son who went to Harvard Business School, and not every start-up will be the next Grab, but every organisation can facilitate internal or external startups. Then help them scale up, stay agile and stay lean. Don't give them too much money and resources though, or you will immediately add bureaucracy and layers of management. Keep them sharp.

Just as parents who give their children too much food, sit them in front of computer games all day, and give them everything want, don't bring up truly independent kids who will thrive in the world, your start-ups won't fly high either if you make life too easy. Keep them on their toes and let them figure things out for themselves. Let them discover the value of money for themselves and you'll see a different behaviours. It works for families and start-ups!

Not all start-ups will survive, but some will, and some will scale up. When scale up time comes, they have the resources, experiences, channels, and the parent organisation's networks; a marketing machine, a sales machine, and technology platforms already in place. They have built up a lot know-how over the years and internal startups can make good use of that.

The Pyramid vs The Swarm

Most pyramid-like structures with clear hierarchies baked in have dependencies baked into the system. In a hierarchy, there's always someone above you who judges you. That creates a level of insecurity, because you're not in the driver's seat. You're not the one making the decisions, people make decisions for you. Whether you're on the factory floor, a manager, a senior executive or even CEO, there are always people or systems above. Shareholders, directors and board members have more say than you do.

Thankfully, swarms are built on completely different principles of equality, not hierarchy. There are leaders in a swarm, but they are situational-based leaders, not fixed ones. One moment someone who is very knowledgeable about a topical subject leads, but when things change another type of leader steps up. In a swarm organisation a different leader will stand up autonomously when needs are known.

These are completely different structures. The new hierarchy isn't based on power, how much you earn, or how long you've worked there. It's based on expertise that's called upon (or not) in certain situations.

When people don't feel comfortable and can't bring their whole being to work, they don't fully develop. That's what is blocking hierarchical organisations from evolving into the next phase.

Dependency isn't just between employee and manager, it's also between departments and organisational layers. There's central management, middle management, IT, HR, accounting, and legal, who each have their own culture and way of working.

More and more of these sub-departments will be automated as they become available as algorithms. Organisations will have fewer people managing departments or complex processes. Inevitably, the need for rigid structures will naturally fade away as we have the technology platforms to manage the complexity for us. Pyramids will crumble over time. Ecosystems such as infrastructure as a service, information as a service, software as a service, and platform as a service will make many layers obsolete.

Swarms - But Flatter

We are 'ultimately heading towards 'organisations as a service'. Soon organisations won't need to focus on managing the complexity of the organisation itself; no HR department, no accountancy - or massively slimmed down versions. Those functions will be woven into the algorithms of a collaboration-based platform. The expensive, high maintenance, complex layers underneath will be managed by smart technology. Such platforms are already emerging.

Evolved organisations will be able to focus their attention on the outside world with full attention on their customers' needs. From a competitive perspective, they will adapt better and faster to their environment than the current pyramid organisations can who still have most of their energy and focus directed inwards. It's understandable, there's a lot of communication to manage, but if that's done by technology, they can turn outwards and evolve into swarm-like structures. They'll be able to continuously monitor the environment and marketplace and adapt to external forces seamlessly. The way we work and the way we learn are two sides of the same evolutionary coin. As organisations become more fluid and self-organising, individuals must become more adaptive and self-directed. The companies of the future will no longer hire for what you know, but for how fast you can learn, unlearn, and relearn. Learning itself becomes the new labour, a lifelong process of inner upgrading that keeps us human in an age of intelligent machines.

The Future of Learning

People are notoriously bad at learning things they aren't interested in, or don't think they are good at. Think of the subject you most hated at school - did you put much effort into it? Of course you didn't!

Organisations will have to think differently about learning. As they evolve towards the inevitable 'organisations as a service', enabled by swarm platforms, we have to start nurturing a deeper appreciation of the natural talents and preferences of individuals. That's the starting point for true cooperation and collaboration.

So, what does that mean in practical terms? Organisations need to understand people better, to enable them to deliver their best work and get fulfilment from it. They will need to know, who you are, what your values are, your strengths and weaknesses, what you like, what your passion is, and what you are good at.

More and more intelligent software tools are emerging to help identify an individual's skills, strengths, values, passions, and purpose. This knowledge can be used to ensure that their role naturally aligns with their true selves. Virtual coaching will help people find their passion and will be enabled by virtual assistants; smart AI-powered dialogue interfaces helping people align with their passion faster. It will become the new normal.

With a starting point of a greater sense of personal direction, AI will help you identify the skills and habits you need to get where you want to go. Technologies that are currently bumping along the bottom of their evolutionary S-Curve will be here sooner than you think. AI, augmented reality, mixed reality, and holographic technologies will soon enable people to learn in a different ways, and enjoy a more personalised learning journey.

That's miles away from old-fashioned learning from books and packing knowledge into your head. Instead, it will be learning by doing, and experiencing things through holographic devices. People will be able to absorb knowledge faster, and because they are learning about things that help them to get where they want to go, the desire to learn becomes a virtuous circle. This is the learning of the future.

Once the passion and the purpose is clear at an individual level, and skills have been developed, you can start matchmaking; connecting groups of people with the same values, intention or purpose. You can create teams based on the personalities and skills needed to achieve specific goals. You can start matchmaking between people with a passion for a specific problems in society too. Maybe you want to engineer physical solutions for moving people around, developing cures for illnesses or cleaning up the oceans. Algorithms and AI can help bring those passionate teams together. Swarm platforms can build personal profiles of individuals that include their values, intentions, standards, and skills - the algorithm can put people together to form instant dream teams. What comes next is for the platform to help create flow within teams so they can fulfil their purpose with as little friction as possible.

Teams that Flow Together Grow Together

If swarm organisations are going to be the future, how do you ensure that hundreds, thousands, or even millions of people can make decisions in real-time, like flocks of birds?

Tools already exist for working with Hive Mind-like technologies, and they use swarm intelligence. They are already in development but still in their infancy, though the strides these platforms are making are huge. With the exponential growth of AI, they will get more powerful very quickly. I am convinced we will be using them to make strategic decisions as a collective in the near future.

Decisions currently made by the CEO or the board of directors will soon be made collectively. The Max Plank Institute demonstrated that swarms are 99% more effective and efficient in preventing and solving problems. We desperately need that kind of wisdom today. To get wise we need to:

1. Give people the opportunity to work at their most powerful with purpose and passions aligned
2. Give them the right skills and training

3. Match them up with other people who can help them achieve defined goals
4. Empower them as a group so they can make collective decisions

Performance Based Ecosystems

Inside organisations bold enough to facilitate such ecosystems, people will excel. They won't need pushing with rewards, bonuses or KPIs. Motivation is built into the system and people will develop themselves by default. They won't need to be forced to do training anymore, they will do that of their own accord. The fruits that come with this will be of huge social value across both the organisation and wider society.

The challenge is that any kind of organisational change process is slow to take off, and for a shift as significant as this one, there will be resistance. With all change, 90% of the energy required is used during the initial stages because it's so hard to change the old ways. So how do you break free from old patterns?

We talked about neural pathways in your brain being like deeply ingrained cart tracks and how breaking out of them takes a lot of energy to get the wheels out, but once you're out, it gets easier and easier. That applies to organisations as it does to individual brains.

People and organisations move faster and faster when they break free of old patterns. Dinosaur companies that don't try hard enough will go the way of the dinosaurs. Thankfully, we have bigger brains than T-Rex did, and technology is helping us evolve at warp speed. To make the most of what's coming we are going to have to unlearn a lot of what got us here.

"Transformation is often more about unlearning than learning."
Richard Rohr

So although the novelty of new is exciting, it's must start with letting go of old processes and patterns. The first 90% energy goes into unlearning. Changing the old culture is possible, but only when we let go of ways that no longer serve us.

Chapter 30

Why Swarms of Micro Entrepreneurs Are the Future of Business

New technology enables ordinary people to do extraordinary things and we are going to see a rise in the number of micro-entrepreneurs because of it. Consider platforms like Uber, Grab, and learning platforms like Udemy and Teachable; the large percentage of service providers are self-employed. They take responsibility for their own income, use their own expertise, resources and knowledge to become part of a bigger ecosystem.

None of this is possible without the app and platform ecosystems that enabled the transformation. Millions have taken charge of their own future thanks to them. The platforms manage complexity and provide an easy-to-use interface for both the micro-entrepreneur and their customers. No matter how niche your interest, someone somewhere will have designed and produced a course that enables you to learn, and connect with others who share your passion. These ecosystems are stacking up with more of them available every day. They support us in focusing on what we enjoy and care about, and push us towards the top of the Maslow pyramid at an ever-increasing rate.

Innovation used to happen primarily in big government labs, aerospace and defence departments, and inside wealthy organisations. Exponentially developed technologies have enabled more individuals and startups to innovate and disrupt, a trend that will accelerate.

Algorithms are the new managers. Think of a symphony orchestra; a group of individuals who all play their instrument with passion. Instead of the conductor being a man with a baton, he's now an algorithm that activates and stimulates the right people at the right time to create a harmonic symphony. I believe this is where organisations are heading; to ecosystems of individuals empowering each other. Take one person out of the orchestra who starts to play alone and it harmony is gone. But put several passionate musicians together, it starts sounding like a harmonious whole again.

Algorithms will bring the right people in, for the right thing, at the right time, at the right place. Technologies like AI are boosting our creativity and productivity. Robots are taking more actions out of our hands. The infinite rise of computing power and storage capacity are designing complicated processes better than people can. Nanotechnology, 3D, 4D printers, smart sensor technologies, and other powerful technologies are getting ever cheaper. Yet people are getting an increased sense of power over what they can do for themselves.

Today, the time from idea to product is getting shorter and shorter. What used to take years can now take just days. Even the lengthy process of getting new drugs to market is getting faster now researchers are using AI to model the effect of drugs on cancer cells, shortening timescales and bringing forward clinical trials.

It's traditional to write a business plan then develop a product. It was expensive too, and took time; you needed a marketing machine, sales channels, and infrastructure. That's been flipped 180 degrees. You can now start selling a product that doesn't even exist yet by using a crowdfunding platform. You just take the idea, pitch it, have a small website or video describing it, how you're going to do it, and how much money you need. Platforms like Kickstarter, Indiegogo, and Fundable persuade future customers to invest a little seed capital. Whether it's ten, or hundreds of thousands of euros, if enough people buy into your idea, you have the starting capital to launch and build out your product or service. There's also the huge advantage of knowing that there are customers for your product at the concept stage and they already have skin in the game. You can be up and running in weeks, not years.

The Rise of Creative Communities

This kickstart business model allows customers to get involved early. In the past, businesses spent years developing products only to find there weren't enough (or any!) customers. Now you can have a continuous co-creation of the product with the people who gave you the money to create something that fills a need.

There's another advantage. That's when you have a great idea, but you don't have all the skills to develop it. Apps to help you find the right people at the right time. InnoCentive, an online platform for inventors, connects you with people with the right skills looking for projects to work on. There are engineers, developers, packaging experts, and marketers at your disposal to help you to get your product to market quickly. Development cycles are dramatically shortened and lead times shortened from years to weeks. The world is speeding up. You can't get away from those S-Curve principles! They are part of nature.

Some of the products coming out of these co-design and co-creation platforms are out performing big brands. Communities are creating cars and mobility solutions; Local Motors 3D was an online community made up of thousands of engineers. In the evenings, they worked together to create a 3D-printed electric car. They worked on a fully autonomous vehicle to move goods and people. Sadly, demand at the time wasn't enough to keep them in business, but the principles that made it happen and the developments they made still exist. The skills, relationships and the technologies still exist too.

New car brands are emerging that put together a car almost off the shelf. These kinds of startups are increasingly system integrators, ordering separate off-the-shelf modules such as batteries, electric motors, a specific modular chassis, or undercarriage. They then print their bodywork on the chassis creating a unique product.

You don't need a team of engineers sitting in an office together with knowledge of materials, products knowledge, and gravitational stress forces. AI generative design and engineering technology will soon evolve into generative design/engineering platforms enabling communities of creatives to engineer a product by just telling the software the constraints, giving ideas for the look of the finished product, telling it what materials to use and the cost constraints. The system then starts to generate and simulate hundreds or thousands (even millions) of variants. Some don't work, and they are discarded. Those that work, are further evolved. A single creative thinker can intervene when they see a variant they like at the right price, and have it printed in 3D knowing that the computer program has taken care of the detailed engineering process and stress testing.

Thanks to these platforms, there's a tidal wave of new tech startups. Communities scattered across the planet are working together on things they are passionate about. There's a resultant explosion of smart devices, smoke detectors, doorbells, thermostats, cameras, robot lawnmowers, vacuum cleaners, drone delivery technology and mobility and logistics solutions. You don't need a company with deep pockets behind you anymore. Just go on line. People are out there waiting to be part of something exciting.

Parallels with Nature and AI Designs

It's no accident that the prototypes coming out of hybrid human-machine-like interactions have a lot in common with natural solutions that have evolved over millions of years. In my keynote I show a type of bracket designed by a person, shown next to a variant designed by AI. The AI version uses less material, handles more stress, and is cheaper to make. I show pictures of products from cars to baby carriers whose AI designed frames show remarkable parallels with the human skeleton using materials structured very like our bones. Nature knows how to give bones more density on the most stressed areas, and so does AI.

"The people have the power. All we have to do is awaken the power in the people."

John Lennon

Technology is going to allow more of us to become micro-entrepreneurs, focussing on doing what we love and helping us pair up with others with complementary skills. Together we can find the right instruments and become part of an orchestra of solutions.

Chapter 31

Organisations Will Become Fluid or Obsolete

How can organisations become more fluid, and what happens if they can't (or won't) make the shift?

Timescales are shortening. The accumulation of ecosystems is happening faster, and each new ecosystem is a stepping stone for the next new development. The first wave of language and agriculture took thousands of years, but the fifth wave (including the rise of the internet, e-commerce, social media, big data, and data analysis tools) took just twenty years. But look at the impact!

The AI wave we are in currently will last around ten to twelve years, but have double the impact of the internet wave that came before it. The coming holographic wave is likely to last just 5 or 6 years and have the double impact again. According to my 7-wave model, we can expect to experience at least six times the technological impact of the internet in the next decade. This level of impact surpasses our current understanding and comprehension.

Each new technology wave connects and empowers even more people, and gets 10 times larger in size and impact. The next waves will force radical change on organisations - whether they like it, or not.

Today, organisations set the tone and people have to adapt to fit in. In the future, it will be the other way round. Currently we spend years learning about a particular profession to practice it inside a conventional organisation. Our entire study time is spent adapting to fit inside a box defined by someone else. Soon, the box itself won't exist.

Organisations will have to adapt to us. They will have to ask what your passion is, what your purpose is, and what goals are you pursuing in life, and how they can help you achieve them. That's at odds with organisations that exist today.

As individuals, we are becoming smarter and more social. We connect and form networks. There will be massive communities of highly motivated people working toward the same goals. We will gradually move away from large commercial organisations as we know them, and move towards purpose-driven social enterprises. There will be a rise in social development goals, global purpose-driven goals like clean drinking water, sustainable energy, equality, and peaceful connection.

As we connect, we can stand against the bad actors who want to use their own goals to control and manipulate us. It's no coincidence that power hungry leaders want to limit information flows, control the media and reduce free speech in social networks. It's their way of maintaining power and keeping the status quo. But technology has become more accessible to more people cheaply, and it's becoming harder for them to stop us doing better together.

This socially based society may feel a long way off, but I believe it's closer than we think. The impacts of the 6th and 7th waves are exceptionally more significant than previous waves. If nature is allowed to take its course the 7th wave end goal is to achieve harmonious global co-creation and collaboration in fluid organisations. All empowered by purpose-driven individuals; swarms of people looking for solutions for a better life. It's going to be ever harder for those in power who don't have our best interests at heart, to stop us.

Commercial organisations will have a tough time dealing with these tech-empowered, intrinsically driven communities. Traditional organisations contain extrinsically motivated people (pay the mortgage, bills, buy food), but organisations with intrinsically motivated people are massively engaged, effective, and productive. Soon technology will be good enough and cheap enough to apply swarm principles on a massive scale. Traditional reptile-like organisations with hard wired behaviour will have to compete with social empathic ones that are fluid and adaptive. It's an unfair match.

Emerging organisational operating systems allow for more decentralised autonomous swarm-like organisations. One early-stage example is Holocracy (or Holospirit), a way to structure organisations differently with smaller self-directed groups of people instead of a top down pyramid model. Management functions are absorbed within smaller self-managing teams. It's a much more organic structure that works more like a human body; everything is connected but different parts of the whole have different functions that self manage; kidneys clean the blood, muscle tissue moves the body but everything knows it's part of a greater whole. There's still marketing and finance, but they know they are part of the something bigger and they are allowed to do their job and interface in a way that helps the whole organisation. As long as the direction of travel is clear and everyone knows where they are going, it has proven to work well.

Holocracy is one of the better-known examples, but there are many ways of structuring that serve different purposes. What they all have in common is a more organic structures that adapts itself afresh each day, continuously evolving with its environment. Organisational adaptation happens through widespread, structured stand-up meetings that aim to resolve any tensions between the different cells. If there is tension between individuals or roles, it gets resolved. If there is tension between team cells, it's resolved. Tension between the primary cell and the outside world gets resolved. It adapts and evolves like natural organisms do. Organisations become living beings, each part ensuring the survival of the whole. That's very different to traditional rigid organisations that need a major reorganisations or restructuring every few years, when parts no longer function well or the external environment has changed. These major restructuring exercises send shock waves throughout and are really bad for morale. People lose their jobs, or get moved to other departments and everyone is in a state of fear. In evolutionary terms, the reactive reptilian brain dominates at such times. Conversely, organisations that use Holocracy as their operating system evolve continuously, fluidly and smoothly. They change a little bit every week instead of having a big shock to the system every five or so years. They continuously adapt to the needs of the outside world and to the people inside. These kind of role-based organisations are still in the early stages and not very smart. Just imagine if AI can help to organise us 10 times more efficiently, just what these organisations might look like.

It can seem as if there's a level of chaos in such organic organisations, but that's not the case because there are precise rules of play. For example, let's use soccer as a metaphor. There's a defined playing field, and within it there are predetermined rules. But within those rules, players can do anything they want. That's how Holocracy-based organisations work; you can't go beyond important rules or limitations, but there is a lot of creative freedom within them. It comes down to the continuous search between control and stability and between flexibility and adaptability. A delicate balance between chaos and order. If organisations can find the right balance, then they enter the flow zone where they are 300-500% more effective than traditional organisations. Studies have demonstrated this time and time again.

In the coming years, organisations will need to search for a balance between the stability of old hierarchical structures and the freedom of the swarm organisations seen in nature. In nature, there is a structure, but we don't yet fully understand its logic and laws.

Most of today's organisations are a long way from being ready. Many are like a container of ice cubes frozen together. Let's call that culture. When ice cubes are stuck together they can't move so there's no interaction, innovation, creativity, and no renewal. If we melt a little, we get more flexible and relaxed, and we can start moving towards a liquid form. Liquid water has virtually no friction. It adapts easily to its environment without putting much energy into the change process. To change the structure of a container of that block of ice cubes you need a lot of force, and the block breaks in a place you don't want it to. That is what happens in organisations when you try to change a rigid pyramid structure by force; it breaks in all the wrong places and people are the victims. Morale drops, and eventually they fall back into their old patterns.

Organisations will become either fluid or obsolete. The world is changing that without fluidity they don't stand a chance.

Intrinsically (purpose) driven communities driven by smart AI will start to compete with the bigger traditional extrinsically (profit) driven organisations. Traditional organisations may hold on for a while because of their size and deep pockets, but smart communities will quickly get the upper hand. There is much friction ahead during the transition.

"The future is fluid. Each act, each decision, and each development creates new possibilities and eliminates others. The future is ours to direct."

Jacque Fresco

Fresco was an architect and social engineer who designed and researched new ways of balancing societies with nature. His ideas were bottom-up, driven from the citizen and enabled by smart technology. His concept of big fluid systems that takes control away from traditional top-down governments and corporate organisations were ahead of their time. Technology is now catching up, and his ideas are becoming ever more possible. The future is fluid and it's up to each one of us to play a part in shaping it.

Chapter 32

Thriving in the Age of Uncertainty

The Cost of Rigidity

Fragile organisations are like glass; they may look strong, but one unexpected blow can shatter them. These organisations resist change and cling to outdated systems and rigid hierarchies, are highly sensitive to disruptions, and even minor challenges can send them spiralling into chaos. Consider a small business that relies on a single supplier. If that supplier faces disruption, the entire operation grinds to a halt. Fragility is not just about breaking under pressure; it's about being unprepared for inevitable shifts that come with a fast-changing world. Fluidity is the counterbalance.

Resilience and Robustness: Bouncing Back Isn't Enough

Some organisations move beyond fragility and become robust or resilient. Robust organisations are like a sturdy tree they can withstand a storm, but if the winds get too strong, they eventually snap. Resilient organisations, on the other hand, are like a rubber band--they stretch and bounce back after being pulled. While this is a step forward, it's still not enough in today's world.

Resilience is reactive, not proactive. It's about surviving, not thriving. Take Kodak, once the leader in the photography industry, collapsed when they failed to adapt to the digital revolution. While Kodak eventually pivoted to new technologies like blockchain, its initial inability to embrace change saw it struggling to regain relevance.

Its name will forever be linked to catastrophic failure for an entire generation of customers.

The Tropophilic Leap: Thriving on Uncertainty

Now, imagine an organisation that doesn't just survive change, it thrives on it. This is the essence of a tropophilic organisation.

The term "tropophilic" comes from the Greek words for "turning" and "love," symbolising a deep embrace of change and uncertainty. These organisations are not just resilient--they are designed to grow stronger and more innovative in the face of disruption.

Tropophilic organisations operate like ecosystems, constantly adapting to their environment. Built on principles of openness, collaboration, and continuous learning instead of rigid hierarchies, they embrace distributed leadership and self-organising teams. Almost like flock of birds moving in perfect harmony, with each individual responding to the group's needs without a central leader.

The SWARM Model: A Blueprint for Becoming a Tropophilic Organisation

So, how do organisations make the leap to tropophilia? One answer lies in the swarm model, inspired by nature that thrive on uncertainty by embracing distributed leadership, rejecting rigid, hierarchical structures and operate as dynamic, self-organising systems.

With leadership distributed, everyone has a role to play, and decision-making is shared. Teams are flat, flexible, and organised around roles rather than rigid job titles. Intrinsic motivation replaces external rewards, fostering a culture of trust and accountability and information flows freely through networked systems, enabling rapid decision-making.

The Human Connection: Lessons for Individuals

This journey isn't just for organisations--it's for all of us. With AI and automation taking off, our ability to adapt and thrive on uncertainty is more important than ever. Tropophilic organisations teach us that change isn't something to fear; it's something to embrace. Just as they thrive on learning, so can you.

Take time each week to learn something new. Surround yourself with people who challenge and inspire you. Collaboration isn't just about working together; it's about growing together and growth often comes from discomfort. Don't avoid challenges, lean into them. What can you learn from the obstacles in your path?

"The more things you own, the more things end up owning you. Travel light."
Tyler Durden

This wisdom applies not just to material possessions but to outdated mindsets and habits. Let go of what no longer serves you and make room for growth.

A Vision for the Future: Tropophilia in the Age of AI

On the brink of the Fourth Industrial Revolution, the need for fluid organisations has never been greater. By embracing the principles of tropophilia, we can create organisations, and lives, that are not just resilient but future-proof. The journey is about humanity's potential to grow and evolve. Are you ready to take the leap?

Chapter 33

The Power of Empowering Eco-Systems

With the changes coming at businesses, how can they harness the power of the next wave? Every wave creates an ecosystem that powers the next wave and in recent years it's the platform ecosystem that has enabled millions of people to reach vast audiences. That reach would have been impossible for an individual or small company in the past. Not anymore.

The first movers in any technology space have the potential to dominate a small emerging market, though not all visionaries make it. Few people remember Laker Airways, the first low-cost transatlantic airline. It went bust but Freddie Laker's airline inspired Richard Branson to launch Virgin Atlantic. Easy Jet for short haul quickly followed. Laker's idea was the catalyst.

At the beginning of each evolutionary wave, a small number of people emerge who see opportunity. They see the potential, recognise a latent need, innovate and make money. In the industrial revolution, it happened in metal, oil, and railroad industries. Industrialist Andrew Carnegie dominated steel, Rockefeller dominated oil and Vanderbilt built railroads. They virtually monopolised their markets at the time, but monopolies rarely last long term. In time society decides that critical infrastructures like railroads can't be owned by a single individual or organisation, critical infrastructure like steel, oil and railroads are made public or became publicly traded companies. It happens in every wave.

In the past waves lasted hundreds of years or decades, but now the process is more abrupt. In the internet wave, Steve Jobs, Jeff Bezos, Larry Page, and Mark Zuckerberg started tech companies that laid down the infrastructure in the information technology field. Like them or not, they took the lead, created the platforms, and developed an ecosystem that others could build on.

In the last 20 years, companies including Apple, Microsoft, Google, and Samsung have created cloud platforms that allow people to develop an app relatively simply. Using free software, developers can then put their apps on the big tech App Stores. It takes little time and money to offer your app to hundreds of millions of people, because the AppStore ecosystem is there.

These tech platforms have big advantages for small developers, and they give a springboard so small start-ups can make a big impact quickly enabling individuals to make money. They float all boats and the platform owners no longer have to create everything themselves. Under pressure from independent developers hosting rates are going down and represent reasonable value. The costs of reaching a massive audience are a fraction of what they were just a couple of years ago.

Though with millions of apps, it's increasingly difficult to get new apps discovered. Just as in the early internet days, companies with a first mover advantage took market share, the same is happening today with apps. It's not enough to have a great product in a store, people have to find it. Today you have to pay search engines to show up in the results. Big tech wins again.

I believe that these infrastructures are too important to be left in the hands of a few powerful organisations. These kinds of platforms need to become more for the public good. How can that happen with most app stores currently under the control of big tech? The answer is that blockchain technology that has the potential to enable a more distributed and democratic ecosystem of new platforms.

More ecosystems will use blockchain-like structures with distributed storage. Like cryptocurrency, instead of being located on central servers of powerful organisations, they are distributed across hundreds of independent servers.

There are alternative platforms in development, though currently still small, are based on decentralised principles so have the ability and capacity to grow quickly. They're not limited to a single company, they are peer-to-peer, separate units connected to each other like the cells in an organism.

The DNA in each of our cells is like an open ledger that stores all genetic transactions and synchronises with billions of other cells in our body. Like Bitcoin and blockchain systems, these early-stage technical solutions are a stepping stone towards organic and decentralised solutions like the DNA in our cells. Nature shows us the way, it always does, and it always will.

This is happening in the crypto currency market as well. So, don't be surprised if you see a strong counter-movement against centralised big tech organisations. Current profit-driven strategies don't always have the best interests of society at heart because financial and political incentives drive their behaviour.

Disruptors - Managing Complexity for Millions

Disruptive companies have built interfaces that are helping millions of people to manage complexity and they are changing entire industries. We've talked about Grab and Uber, and there's a similar effect with property rental platform Airbnb that's democratised room lettings and disrupted the traditional hotel business. Anyone can offer a room, apartment, or house for rent to a worldwide audience. Customers have greater choice and property owners don't need their own platform - which would be uneconomic to build just to let out the spare room once in a while.

You no longer have to book an expensive hotel for hundreds per night, you can rent something that suits through via Airbnb for a relatively low cost. It's turned the hotel industry upside down with thousands of jobs lost, but thousands more new AirBNB businesses have been created. It's so successful that it's created huge downsides though, with properties empty during off-season, negative effects on housing affordability and an influx of short-term rentals changing the character of neighbourhoods.

Building Trust

There's another trend that's going to quickly have an impact on co-creation platforms. If you're collaborating online and you've never met someone, how do you know if you can trust them and do business with them safely?

Platforms do some of the work for you by holding money in escrow until the work is done, but there are still holes in the system. In an online world where hacking, false identity and scams are endemic, we need ways to improve security. Technologies like blockchain will help, making it possible to transact with strangers safely. Looking someone in the eye can be replaced by smart technology.

Blockchain allows you to view the track record of an individual inside the blockchain network of transactions. How trustworthy are they? have they kept their agreements in previous collaborations? What level of quality do they deliver?

We use reviews and recommendations, but they are easily faked. But we can make this watertight via the blockchain, allowing for ad-hoc collaborations with people you've never met. We can now do financial transactions with strangers through smart blockchain contracts, making conditional payments based on prearranged agreements that would generally have to go through a notary.

Evolution is primarily about the empowerment created when new ecosystems can deliver more options. This has happened in every wave - and inside every S-Curve. Each ecosystem is a springboard for the next. It happened in the industrial revolution, the telecom revolution, and now we are seeing it happen with big tech too. The timelines are getting shorter, organisations and communities are getting exponentially bigger, and more influential, in exponentially shorter timeframes. timeframes.

"Leaders become great not because of their power, but because of their ability to empower others."

John Maxwell

The organisations and technologies of the future will connect and empower a lot of people. In the social media / internet wave, many big tech companies have grown from zero to billion dollar companies. As long as they have empowered people, they've been successful. I believe that in the AI wave, and the coming holographic wave, organisations will become multiples of the of current big tech companies in size and impact.

Big tech in the 6th and 7th waves will no longer be managed by a few individuals. They'll be so powerful that they can only be governed by the collective or swarm. Their power will be too significant to rest in the hands of a few. If they become owned and governed by the collective, we will play by very different rules.

Your Purpose is Your Future

With so many jobs being automated by AI and robotics many of us will be pushed toward our purpose. In parallel there will be more empowering ecosystems that will empower people to pursue their passions. Through new artificial intelligence-powered platforms with user-friendly voice interfaces, more of us will move from traditional hierarchical systems to more swarm-like organisations that are more about equality and personal passions, and less about filling the pockets of shareholders or the CEO.

"The meaning of life is to find your gift. And the purpose of life is to give your gift away."

Pablo Picasso

So, find out what your gift is. Ask yourself what makes you happy. Ask where you get your creative inspiration from.

Develop that into a product or service, share it with others on the new platforms, and create value. You never know where it might lead you.

Part IV - AI's impact on Skills and Talents

Chapter 34

Identifying New User Interfaces

Our traditional mindset and worldview has already been outpaced. We need to adapt quickly. So, how do we do that? First, we need to understand the flaws of the dominant Western worldview, and grasp how we can unlock new options.

Our society is dominated by thinking derived from our left-brain hemisphere powering our rationality and logic, heavily biased towards subjects like mathematics, chemistry, and physics. Our Western educational systems and economics have focused on developing this left hemisphere, and it's successfully powered the industrial age. We are driven and dominated by scientific insight which have brought many good things, but it's unlikely to be the only thing that takes us forward. Tomorrow's world will become too complex to manage with old style thinking.

In a stable world changing slowly, it's possible to manage complexity by dividing a complex problem into sub-problems and chunk down further into tiny granular problems. Almost all traditional hierarchical organisations work like this.

The left-brain approach suggests that solving the small issues, you can solve the big issue, but this approach easily misses the fact that the broader problem is part of something much bigger. Overarching problems are rarely static, and often aren't in your control either and they continually evolve, usually at a faster pace than you can solve the sub-issues underneath. You get further and further behind the big problem rather than getting ahead of it.

Splitting broader issues into smaller sub-issues means you constantly come up against new complex problems that need even more specialisation and isolation. You end up generating more sub-issues than you started with!

In a world that is continuously changing exponentially, solving sub-issues has lost its usefulness. Take medicine. Scientists study the workings of the body by dividing it into anatomically smaller pieces; organs, tissues, cells, proteins, and molecules. We know what each minor part does, but it's easy to loose sight of the fact that each part is an integral part of a larger whole. We know what diseases do to us, but in many cases, we still have no idea of the underlying causes. As a result, our medical system practices symptom suppression on a massive scale.

It's happening in politics and business too. We are stuck in an old-fashioned way of thinking with global multidimensional crises unfolding around us in food, energy, health, finance and resources. Hierarchically organised systems are cracking everywhere, symbolising the end of the old-thinking era. Our current way of thinking and managing complexity is holding us back.

So how can we combine our current scientific way of thinking with a more holistic one?

The answer is to zoom out so we can view all parts of problems and see them in the broader context of one integral whole, in the same way as we look at living ecosystems. We don't lose the details, we just make them smaller relative to the whole picture. That's almost of reverse of what we do currently. Now more than ever, we need a mindset that sees the bigger picture and the underlying causes, rather than just the symptoms.

"The major problems in the world are the results of the difference between how nature works and how people think."
Gregory Bateson

Bateson was a revolutionary thinker. Much of his work changed the way we solve problems. An anthropologist, social scientist, and linguist, his work spanned many disciplines. I believe he was ahead of his time when he said that Western scientific thinking was unnatural and was not how nature or the universe solves problems. I agree. We need to learn to think from a holistic and ecological perspective. If we can do that, many societal issues will solve themselves.

Chapter 35

The 6th Wave - Artificial Intelligence

When we talk about AI, many people think of the movie The Terminator, where Skynet's AI starts making its own decisions and decides to wipe out humanity. Fortunately, we are still far away from that. Whether it will ever get there depends entirely on how we deal with AI. At the moment we are still on a very different level of AI.

Remember Clippy, the supposedly helpful (and very annoying) paper clip from Microsoft Office? It was anything but intelligent and always appeared at the wrong moment, usually when your document was about to crash. Clippy would pop up, the system would crash, and you'd lose everything. Three or four hours work up in virtual smoke.

Most of us don't really understand the intelligence of computers. It's a box under your desk that often doesn't do what you want it to do. It's anything but intelligent. But the domain of AI is different. In big Tech today, every major technology company is betting heavily on the development of neural networks or self-learning computers.

Consider Tesla. It's seen by many as a car company, but in reality, it's an AI company with a car product. Tesla cars are full of cameras, radar technology and other sensors feeding back and interpreting all the data. The information and camera images allow it to drive autonomously. Getting you from A to B has moved from solving a transport problem, to solving an information problem.

For fully autonomous motoring you need special neural chips, which are now in production. Recently Apple released the M5 chip, one of the fastest consumer computer chips available at the time, built to process data from advanced neural networks. More and more AI is used inside our operating systems on everyday laptops and PCs already. AI now recognises faces in the pictures we store. Google uses TensorFlow Processing Units (TPU's) in their data centres, chips specifically built to run and process neural networks.

Moore's law, stating that computers generally double in performance every 12 to 18 months, is already outdated here too. Nvidia's AI chips are doubling in price performance ratios every 6 to 8 months. That's a quadrupling in speed every year; the doubling is already outdated.

Current mainstream processors are still based on silicon and transistor technology, but there is a whole new S-curve of technology eager to start. The IBM Neurosynaptic TrueNorth chip with brain inspired architecture has a million programmable neurons that can make new connections based on what it needs to do, adjusting internal routing based on the task. That's closer to how our brains works than any older generation chips.

MemComputing INC. has a MEMCPU chip, a chip with storage and processing woven into one unit, making it work much faster. Normally, a processor takes instructions from memory and the hard drive, and when it's done, it sends data back and writes it again - continuously writing back and forth. But when memory and processing are together, as in our brains, it's faster and more efficient. Even more advanced technologies that are still under wraps are coming soon.

Technology gets more like our biology every day. That's hardly surprising when you understand how well nature solves complex problems. We would be wise to learn from that.

The Holy Grail of computing is quantum computing and it is being heavily pursued by many companies. The first quantum computers are coming out of the labs and into commercial use already, a sign that the technology is maturing rapidly. Aerospace and defence are the first big users, with universities rapidly following on. I believe quantum will be mainstream in the next five to ten years.

Are we at the point where AI is truly mainstream yet? Well, it's become so cheap and powerful that it's appearing in all kinds of applications. There's already enough computing power to process neural network data that's very computationally intensive, there are algorithms that can run them. Ten years ago, you needed a data centre of servers just to process what the chip in your phone does today.

Billions of dollars of capital are flowing into new AI startups. Huge amounts of data has been gathered over the last 20 years and internet content is food for these systems. AI needs lots of data to learn from. Layered over that there's the human talent. For multiple decades people have been working on neural networks. Many of the brightest minds on the planet are working on them. Now that the preconditions are in place, AI will fly.

In previous waves, when there were nails, hammers and planks, people built barns. Now the raw material of AI, chips, capital, data, and computing power are converging. The ecosystem is so powerful we are seeing one application after another. You can almost take any problem, bolt AI onto it, and you have a new startup.

Predictable Evolution

AI (synthetic intelligence is perhaps a better term) goes through the same phases as a human baby, but much faster. Computers are already better than humans at recognising pictures, patterns and images, and better at interpreting sensor information. They can take millions of variables, and make decisions.

When you put image recognition, cameras, and sensors into a car, drone, or robot, they can already navigate the environment pretty safely. Algorithms understands language which takes huge computational power due to its complexity - everyone use different words in different contexts. Once computers really understand that well, then they will understand the fabric of society. Everything we do is based on language and non-verbal communication and computers are learning this at breakneck speed. They don't just learn one language either, they can learn hundreds.

When computers fully understand language, they will understand our societal context; from our emails, our agreements, legal contracts, how we talk to our smart devices, and what we ask our search engines. When computers understand all that, they can start making decisions. At first, they will make decisions with us. Later they will make decisions for us.

AI is powering many applications we don't even notice. Most Apple smartphones use AI-powered facial recognition based on neural networks. That one app doesn't just have the capability to recognise, it can recognise your food too. Point the camera at a plate, and it recognises French fries or sausage. It can estimate how many grams of food is on your plate, the nutrients and fats present and if it's wise to eat it given your diet. Soon the smartest dieticians in the world will be in your pocket for 9,95 per month.

There's a Google app that takes a picture of the back of your eye, and using neural networks recognises subtle patterns of your veins. If the vein patterns in your eye deviate, then that same deviation is also likely to be present in the vein patterns around your heart. In the future these AI apps could refer you directly to a cardiologist. Today a diagnosis still requires a CT or MRI scan and a hospital admission, but soon you'll only need an internet connection and your smartphone. Algorithms driving apps like this are turning industries upside down.

When you put sensors and cameras of that quality and sensitivity into a car, autonomous cars will become reality. Regulations will be playing catch up for years. Drive-AI was recently acquired by Apple. In the demonstrations the lady doing the 'driving' doesn't touch the controls. Currently, that's far from ideal because we don't know how it will perform when it's dark, raining or snowing. Developments are in the early stages at the moment, but the sector is accelerating exponentially. The doubling has already begun.

Tesla now has around 5 million cars on the road. Every car encounters and learns from new situations that are uploaded to the Cloud and shared with all the other cars. Each car learns a particle of the available variables, but combine all the learning into one networked knowledge-base and the cars learn 5 million times faster than a person.

It is likely to take a while before they are extremely safe, but once they are, they will replace driver-controlled vehicles quickly.

Levels of AI

Currently there are several levels of AI and what we see most is AI Narrow Intelligence. For example, the intelligence that can drive a car is very sophisticated, but very narrow. You wouldn't get far if you asked it to bake a cake or read a book, but it's pretty good at driving a car.

Narrow intelligence AI can interpret X-rays and recognise tumours. That's a very small piece of intelligence that goes very deep, but don't ask it to vacuum your house.

Then there's a middle more general form of intelligence gently emerging in LLM's (large language models) like ChatGPT, Google Gemini and Claude from Anthropic. These AI's have general knowledge about many things. This middle intelligence needs an extensive array of knowledge, and it needs to understand the intention and context behind the question being asked. To give great answers it needs to understand the context from a previous question, sentence or even conversations that took place on a different day. The human brain does that automatically, but for machines that's an extremely complex challenge.

The third form is Super-intelligence. That's the one that people are afraid of. It's a million times smarter than a human. The nightmare scenario is that one day it will decide people are a bunch of useless creatures who are destroying everything and they aren't needed anymore, and we will exterminate them. Personally, I don't see it that way.

I see AI in the Cloud as having similar qualities to our neocortex brain, there to serve the rest of our body and increase the quality of life and survival of the society of cells that comprises it. AI in the Cloud will do the same thing, if it's used for the right purposes.

We need as many people with clear and positive ethics in our design process as we have computer geniuses that can design the functionality of the machines. AI should be truth seeking by design and be used in the right way and for the right purpose. We haven't reached super intelligence yet. It will probably take another seven to fifteen years, but if we do, then we'll have such intelligence at our disposal we will be able to do things that we can't even dream about today.

Developments are moving fast. Google's DeepMind division is working on a new type of intelligence that uses reinforced learning, capable of learning from its own mistakes. That's how humans learn.

A traditional AI algorithm feeds hundreds of thousands (even millions) of examples; it's brute force learning. DeepMind's new system learns from its own mistakes making it much faster than traditional AI.

The DeepMind team connected the new AI to different computer games without giving any further instructions. The AI could play better than any human alive within a few hours. They challenged it to play GO, the most challenging game on earth where you place black and white stones on a checkerboard. There are more possible moves than there are atoms in the known universe. Playing GO involves intuition and creativity, and until recently consensus opinion believed that computers wouldn't be able play it successfully for a long time. But when DeepMind pitted its computer against the GO world champion Lee Sedol, the computer won four games out of five. Since then, it has made new breakthroughs and is winning against whole teams of the world's best players, 100% of the time. That demonstrates the speed of development.

The next big challenge is to be able to apply this kind of AI to solve health-related issues.

AI is a powerful technology, and like the atomic bomb, we must deal with it responsibly. Stephen Hawking said "Success in creating AI would be the biggest event in human history, unfortunately, it might also be the last, unless we learn how to avoid the risks." Used with the wrong intentions or goals, it could be our downfall.

I see AI like raising a child; put that child in a positive environment and teach it good things, and give it good examples of contribute positively to society when it grows up. Our genius developers will need to work on doing that part too

Chapter 36

AI - The User Interface For The Masses

The impact of the 6th wave will be massive and we will see new user interfaces enabled by AI that will simplify complexity accumulated in previous waves.

All the preconditions to kickstart the exponential growth of AI are already here. Even the smart algorithms themselves are being developed by AI. We are entering the 6th wave, the exponential part of the AI S-curve where the AI ecosystem is becoming more robust.

Google, IBM, Microsoft, Amazon, and others are already offering their AI development libraries for free or next to nothing to everyone allowing developers to create advanced applications in even fewer steps. Those libraries are building blocks, like LEGO, allowing people to quickly develop new products and new applications. There will be more spare bedroom start-ups than ever! Bolt all those ecosystems together and they enable a new concept for a tech startup to get going at record speed.

AI is moving into manufacturing, accountancy, legal services and consumer-related industries like e-commerce and healthcare. The landscape of startups is growing exponentially. For example, accountancy is all about numbers, and jobs are based on spreadsheets with numbers. Spreadsheets are about pattern recognition and AI is currently better than people at that. It can detect numerical trends, helping companies to better manage their finances and workforce. There will be an explosion of virtual private accountants and bankers to help you manage your finances. We're already seeing it happening.

Look at how many large banks and insurance companies are closing branches and laying off thousands of people. Services are going digital at an exponential rate as more and more processes are automated by smart algorithms.

In the legal sector AI algorithms can read millions of legal documents in seconds and will be able to detect if your plans, contracts, or proposals, are legally correct or not.

In healthcare, AI applications already interpret sensor information; your heartbeat, blood pressure and more. Assessing those things together and extracting minor nuances from the data, gives you a snapshot of your health and can predict problems before they happen. Healthcare applications alone are almost endless.

Robotisation

AI can turn dumb machines into smart autonomous ones; drones, robots, and autonomous cars are at the forefront today, but there will be thousands more machines that AI will revolutionise.

Drones are being used for good things, not just wars. They are delivering medication to remote areas of Africa. In 2022 a new born baby was saved after life-saving suction tube was delivered by drone within 20 minutes, the baby's airway was cleared and a life saved. 75% of blood products are delivered by drones in Rwanda, and they are being used to prevent malaria across the continent by spraying larvicide into water where deadly mosquitos breed.

Autonomous robots are much better at people for doing boring, repetitive work in large factories and distribution centres. They don't get tired, bored or make mistakes at the end of a long shift. It's inevitably going to have a significant impact and cause turmoil in many economies.

Where AI is ultimately going to make the biggest difference, is that it's going to make technology more human. We've had to adapt to technology until recently. We've had to learn programming languages, take courses and train to operate it. But now technology is so smart that it's adapting to us.

We are already seeing better user interfaces implemented in cars, smartphones, tablets, and smart speakers. AI is making connecting with technology more convenient and natural.

Connecting Old and New

Many AI startups are working on multiple intelligent interfaces, creating and intuitive dialogue layers between old legacy systems. In the previous wave, we built large, unwieldy systems like CRM, ERP, databases that weren't compatible with each other. If you put an interactive layer of technology on top of that with AI, you could consult it by simply asking questions, allowing you to get answers from all those legacy technology layers underneath, without having to rebuild them.

These developments will make technology even easier, allowing more people to work with it. The threshold for training and experience needed will get ever lower. Tech giants are working hard to deploy natural dialogue interfaces to ever more devices and systems and they learn extremely fast. You can already ask your smart assistant to turn off the lights, close the curtains and turn on Netflix.

In a few years we will have more interactions and transactions using voice dialogue systems. Imagine you run out of milk and sugar, and say, "hey, ChatGPT (or Gemini, or Alexa), I'd like to have that product, just like last time, and the assistant responds "I can do that for you". Then, it's looks for the cheapest option and orders it. You won't even have to go to a website or app for a particular retailer anymore. This kind of tech and the companies developing it are quickly creating new interfaces that will take away a lot of today's complexity.

Voice and facial authentication are developing rapidly. Currently, with most phone-based banking, there's a ton of security to go through before you can do anything. With improved voice and facial recognition technology, we can dispense with that and ask your bank to do a transaction easily. In the near future, if you go for dinner with your family, you'll be able to talk to your device and tell it that you would like to go to a particular restaurant, ask it to reserve a table for five, and once it knows you habits it will prompt you and ask if you want order a cab, and if you want theatre tickets afterwards. AI will take care of it all, based on your preferences.

Barriers Are Dropping Away

Currently, speaking and doing business with people in other countries is still hampered by language and cultural barriers. That's largely already being solved. Apple recently launched the 'AirPod Pro 3' earbuds that have a real-time AI translation functionality that goes way beyond just listening to music or podcasts. They allow you to speak to someone in a foreign language! If the other person has the same Apple earbuds, you can just have a normal conversation like there are no language differences at all. This can already be done in multiple languages in real-time. In conference programs like Google Meet, multiple different languages can already be used in real-time. These developments are moving forward at lightning speed. Very soon AI-powered technology might facilitate all the languages and all the dialects in the world. In addition, people will hear your original voice, not a computer generated one. That's going to be an interesting challenge for security for banking and medical conversations, for example.

WaveNet, a Google subsidiary, has a vocal speaking library of musician John Legend that allows your Google Assistant to use John's voice. It's almost indistinguishable from reality. You can do that yourself with an AI algorithm that uses your voice data to convert your voice into the voice of you speaking in a different language.

That call with your Chinese-Mandarin friend - it's going to be able to convert your side of the conversation into Mandarin using your natural sounding voice so your friend hears your voice in their language. This is already being used with deep-fake video.

Most of us have seen videos where Trump or Obama says something that's clearly false with a voice generate using AI with the lips automatically synchronised. It will be almost impossible to see that someone is not really speaking that language as technology improves.

The next step will be when we're no longer talking to a speaker or an icon on your phone, but to a virtual human-like character. We'll be able to compose that character however we want. This human-like avatar will have its own neural network and synthetic nervous system. He or She will be able to recognise your emotions from your face, and react to your facial expressions and your emotional state allowing for much more natural dialogue. Whether you're talking to a mobile screen or to a character makes a huge difference in how you formulate your words and sentences. It affects the tone you use and what emotions you experience. The more we express ourselves, the more computers will be able to understand what we really mean.

The words we say, the body language we display and our tone of voice can completely change the meaning of what we say. Companies like Effectiva (whose systems already excel at recognising human emotions and states) can capture your emotions and expressions and make sense of the context of your communication. If you say something and make an incongruous facial expression, it knows to ask if you are being serious or joking. AI-powered dialogue systems will learn to understand these nuances.

When we put all those things together; emotions, language and expressions, you will have far more natural conversations with technology lowering the threshold for interacting with technology even further. People with disabilities, children, the elderly, and others who might currently struggle, will soon feel included.

Every wave has its advantages, and its disadvantages. As technology becomes more powerful the potential for abuse increases. For example, when technology understands language and context (say of an email or digital message) it can be used for mass surveillance. That's what security agencies are doing today. In some countries, facial recognition and all kinds of communications between people are monitored. It's one of the dangers of AI and we are wise to be aware of it and make sure that it's developed from an ethical, moral perspective, as well as just a technological one.

AI will take a massive empowering step by making technology more human. And when technology becomes more human, it has more impact. We can do more, with less.

As you know, each solution created by an evolutionary wave creates the next problem to be solved. Security of data our personal digital identity will be the next big challenge.

"Today a group of twenty individuals empowered by the exponentially growing technologies of AI and robots and computers and networks and eventually nanotechnology can do what only nation-states could have done before."

Peter Diamandis

Diamandis is right. A small group of passionate individuals using these potent technologies can do things that only governments could do until now. That power is within reach of individuals and startups, and it's changing the game. When we get to the 7th wave, we'll be even more empowered. We are in exciting times.

Chapter 37

The 7th Wave - Holograms and New Realities

With the acceleration of AI in the 6th wave, we need to start thinking about the 7th wave. What will it be, and what will its impact be?

Like all waves that have come before it, the 7th wave will have a massive effect on society, organisations, and on our personal lives and it will be centred around holographic technologies.

Since the advent of the Internet, we have social media platforms, better search engines, e-commerce, education platforms, mobile banking, and all kinds of peer-to-peer matchmaking and sales platforms. It has radically impacted us in less than a generation. The 7th wave will replicate that impact again, but even more profoundly.

If you lived through the 80's, it was difficult to imagine the impact that the internet would have, but now it's just part of life and we are getting used to AI as part of our daily lives. So far we haven't experienced the early days of the holographic wave. When we look at the Internet today, it's an abstract representation on a flat 2D- screen you view through your smartphone, tablet or computer. We see it through a very small window with text, graphics, videos and animations, and that's about it. It's an abstract form of the digital world.

Now, imagine an Internet that is all around you. No longer just on a flat-window into our digital world but part of your outer reality. That's what the 7th wave is about. If you take AI and add holographic technology, you get the Spatial Web.

As AI starts to understand more of the world around us it's laying the foundation for the next wave; a mixed and augmented reality that comes off the screen and into your wider life.

To imagine that, we first have to understand reality itself - and that is what AI is doing now. By fully understanding the real world, AI can serve as a bridge between the real and virtual world and we will see them blend together. It will be so real that will be hard to tell the difference between the two.

We live in a common reality we call our physical world, perceiving it through our senses: our eyes, ears, touch, and sense of smell. Those senses together determine how we perceive our environment. It feels immersive. We know we are in it, which gives us the feeling of presence. The more senses we engage, the more immersed we are, and the more we can focus on what we are doing.

7th wave technologies will help us to create a sense of presence in the virtual world, fooling our brains to such an extent that they will accept the virtual world as if it's a tangible reality. I believe that the dividing line between virtual and real is likely to disappear in the next five to ten years.

Alternative Reality Is Coming

The emergence of the Spatial Web will herald a normalisation of an alternative reality. That's its defining characteristic. No longer will the internet be trapped on a 2D flat-screen, it will be all around us in 3D and will impact everything we do. We have lived with 2D internet for a generation. We will experience a completely new form of reality.

The reality we know now is tangible. A world we have known through the ages that has changed very gradually. For a few years, we've had limited access to virtual reality, a virtual world separated from our real one. It's been marginalised to gaming and online collaboration platforms, with a limited number of people exposed to it. To enter this virtual world, you need a VR mask, like a scuba mask with TV screens that take you into an isolated world. But people are social beings. We want to connect with our outside world and with others. The next wave is going to combine these two worlds. We will be able to mix the real world and the virtual one through holographic technology and create a seamless blend between the real and the virtual.

Currently VR masks are expensive and clumsy, but they are becoming smaller, cheaper and better. They still take us into an isolated world that allows us to imagine we are doing things that are impossible in the real world. For example, you can almost believe you are flying or travelling through space. As virtual reality becomes better and cheaper, people will get ever more creative with it. It's will be a peek around a door of completely new solutions and applications that we haven't considered yet.

This is the move towards the next wave of blended reality, mixed reality and extended reality; mixing the real world with virtual photorealistic elements floating in virtual space, but linked to our real space. So, if you turn your head, the virtual objects stay where they are. If you place a virtual cup on a real table and turn your head and then turn it back, the cup is still in exactly the same spot, just like in the real world. This is called spatial or holographic computing.

Information will be presented in a way that is very easy for your brain to process. Your visual cortex is extremely fast and very good at processing that kind of information, far faster and more easily than it can read text. You can take in and use information in a faster way using 3D. Our real world is already 3D so your brain is ready, even if the technology to deliver it isn't quite powerful enough yet, but it's coming.

The 7th wave has appeared, it's a little cumbersome, but it's here. New headsets are being released offering mixed reality as well as virtual reality. New generation of masks have cameras, allowing virtual objects to be combined with the images from the real world's camera image with a resolution close to that of the human eye. The images so good your eye can no longer distinguish individual pixels, so your brain assumes reality.

Apple is already building devices like the Apple Vision Pro capable of projecting virtual humans into your real environment. That virtual person could soon be your private banker, accountant, teacher, mentor or coach. They will be projected into your real world, and even able to walk around your house. If they stand behind your sofa, you will see the sofa in front of them. They will be able to walk around your furniture and your brain won't know the difference. If a virtual object is put somewhere in the picture, it stays neatly on the table or floor without sinking through it.

With AI this powerful, and the sensors to map the real world allowing our devices to understand the 3D scanned space, we will be able to mix the real world with the virtual one seamlessly. Combine that with increasing computer power, we will soon be able to generate photorealistic 3D environments in realtime and paste them into the real world.

Industry experts predict that this will roll out into a $19 billion industry within just four to five years. Every major tech giant is working on applications focused on delivering this experience to millions of users.

There are rumours that Apple will launch Apple Glass in one to two years. Replacing a clunky mask with a pair of designer glasses with sensors, processors, cameras with projection technology incorporated inside. How long will it be before there's a collaboration between your smartphone that allows you to project your own choice of images onto the screen inside your glasses? You will be able to interact with the Internet in a more natural way than is currently possible.

META is already working on Virtual Reality (VR) masks than create 3D generated avatars of people having a conversation. They are so realistic that it's difficult to tell the difference between the real people and virtual ones. That will enable you to have natural conversations with people on the other side of the world as if they are in the same room. If we are working in a swarm organisation, we will be able to connect with individual swarm members and see them as if they sitting next to us.

Large companies like Meta and Apple have almost bottomless pockets to fund this kind of research. They see the future in transforming their platforms into a visual ones, where you see virtual representations of real people. When that happens, the Internet won't be flat, it will be part of the world around you. New technologies will make that possible.

The latest generation of iPhones has a LiDAR scanner, tiny sensors that measures how long light takes to travel to a certain point, allowing them to measure the distance from the sensor to the environment. With that, the phone can make a detailed 3D scan of the environment. If you add AI to that, your phone will be able to match that 3D scan with the virtual world.

These technologies will give us a completely different Internet. Unlike a zoom call where you see people shrunk to the size of a postage stamp, they will be in front of you, lifelike and full size. Your brain will hardly be able to distinguish between what is real and what's virtual. The more real that becomes, the easier the interface becomes between people and technology gets.

I've seen and experienced several of these technologies and to my surprise, my body responded differently than I expected. Even though I knew it was fake, it only took a few seconds for my brain to take it for granted that it was real. Imagine what would happen if we could even get rid of the glasses and masks! I believe that we will eventually because of a new field called light field technology.

I was in New York a while ago and people from a company were telling me they were developing next generation light field technology. It's still secret and very early stage, so I can't name names, but what I witnessed was the projection of photorealistic objects in space, without wearing a mask or glasses. It made the interaction with the virtual world feel so natural! It's going to revolutionise everything. You won't have to adapt to technology by putting something on your head because light field technology makes many things possible at once.

Imagine sitting in your living room, with a window frame created in front of you. Behind the window, is a three-dimensional experience of the world beyond, or a conversation with someone who is standing there - with no mask. Light field technology will make the dividing line between the real and virtual world almost disappear, without you having to adapt to the technology, making the learning curve is virtually zero. You already know how the real world works, so you will know instantly how the virtual world works.

One of the creators of this kind of light field technology, told me;

"Our main goal is to create experience that you cannot distinguish from reality, visualising our ideas in the most natural way, just understanding the fundamentals of how the things should work and look"'.

It won't be long before we will be able to share our creative expression in a universal language. It's like the difference between writing a document and sharing it with ten people (all of whom will have a different interpretation of the words and meaning) and showing a hologram that all ten people can interact with. Just imagine how that's going to speed up the development process of ideas for every industry on the planet. It will result in a gigantic boost of innovation that will move us through to yet another wave.

Real - Just Added To

What if everyone on earth could interact with each other and co-create in massive online communities? The Augmented Reality coming with the 7th wave will bring interfaces so universal and easy to use that everyone will be able to use it almost without thinking. As more of our communication becomes visual, we will be able to make massive steps towards further evolution of mankind.

With holograms we will interact very differently with our environment and with other people. Technology, our environment, and humans will merge more and more. Yet, paradoxically we are also moving towards a world where those environments can be different for each person. So, if you're walking down a street, you might see different things and different billboards than I would see walking down the same street. That already happens online. It's perhaps a bit surreal now, but it's what's coming.

Our personalised reality will have virtual objects projected to our brains that are indistinguishable from the real thing. Imagine walking through a city decorated based on your preferences, the things you like or find beautiful. Next, we will start interacting with it. This vision is an early stage vision of something called voxels; volumetric light objects that we can interact with our hands. It's just the beginning of what will be possible.

We are only at the very beginning of the curve of the 7th wave. One of the things that's been holding us back from having life-like 3D conversations in digital form is the computing power required to capture human movement. To collect the data to recreate CGI of a moving person, you need a motion capture suit so the computer can capture natural movement and superimpose a new image on top. With new camera and sensor technology that will be gone. Advanced AI powered cameras will scan your body and facial movements and advanced AI algorithms will translate the data into a complete 3d model of your body with bones, muscles, and everything in it in - in real-time. This virtual representation of you will be able to communicate and cooperate in a totally new way with other people on line.

Microsoft is working on a technology they call Holoportation enabling you to interact with a full-size hologram of a person using their HoloLens technology. One of their demonstrations shows a woman standing on stage who has given a keynote in English, who instructs her holographic Avatar to give that exact same keynote in Japanese using her natural movements and expressions.

In my first book, Humanification, I wrote about the digital double, a digital representation of ourselves in the virtual world. It was a prediction that's coming true. We will all have a digital double that looks and thinks the same as you do, and makes the same decisions. You will be able to be present in multiple places simultaneously on the Internet to deliver your added value. For example, you will be able to inspire people, help people, coach people, and you won't have to do it all yourself. The recipient will feel like you have been with them one on one. That will be a game changer.

A virtual AI version of you will be able to learn continuously from you too. Every interaction you have with it makes it smarter. We're moving towards a world where we will be free again, yet omnipresent at the same time.

Exponential growth by doubling is already happening. The stadium is filling with water fast. AI generated 3D environments and characters with a level of visual quality is on a par with high-end Hollywood movies with computer-generated special effects. We are very close to having fully immersive environments with immersive sound that's so realistic our brain takes it as reality.

Until recently, scanning 3D environments was expensive, but now a drone can fly over an area and scan it using advanced 3D sensors to create a 3D model so realistic you can walk through it. That technology is getting so cheap it's becoming within reach of creative individuals. What was only seen in big-budget Hollywood movies is already possible in real-time for everyone. Like an artist, you can create weather systems with realistic clouds and manipulate them and grant them magic powers allowing you to create virtual environments going beyond our current imagination. That's the world we're about to enter, one of unlimited possibilities and unlimited space; a parallel universe almost where we can all rediscover who we are and what we want to do.

In my opinion, nothing beats the real world. However, I think these virtual worlds will make it possible for us to work together on a massive scale. In previous chapters, we have seen that the idea of swarms give us the possibility to work together seamlessly. AI and hologram technologies will make them possible. If time and place becomes less relevant it will change the way we solve problems together, how we run society, our organisations, and how we create products and services.

If we start doing more in a virtual world, we will need fewer resources, less travelling, building materials, and create less pollution. We'll become more sustainable with more circular economies and better use of resources.

The billions of cells in our body can all communicate with each other at the speed of light via biophotons, and that's where we humans are going next. We will be able to communicate with each other at the speed of light with holographic tools on a global scale.

You won't have to gain your knowledge from books, you will experience it virtually. You'll be able to learn to play piano by seeing your virtual hands playing the keys. Your brain thinks these are your real hands and will create the neural networks needed to play. Then all we then have to do is condition our bodies to use those neural networks. The U.S. Defense Department is already using these kinds of technologies. They've found out that those systems help people learn skills thirty times faster than before. Albert Einstein said:

'The only source of knowledge is experience'
Albert Einstein

You need to actually experience something to really know about it. You can read about it, but you only really experience it when you have felt it and seen it. Only then does it become deeply engrained in your neural pathways. Soon you will be able to create almost any experience you can think of. We are going to be able to experience, design, create and simulate so many things. That's exponential growth for the human race..

Part V - AI's impact on Humans

Chapter 38

Being Human in the 4th Industrial Revolution

Outdated Education Systems

We are still educating people for a world that no longer exists. Our entire educational system and economy has, for the last 100 years, been focused on people learning the skills required to perform repetitive and routine tasks, teaching people to follow procedures and produce consistent results.

But technology will soon augment or replace many hard skills we have been educated to rely on. Professional roles that were once considered immune to the march of the robots will be affected and people are already feeling the effects, and they don't know what to do about it.

We will have to find a way to stay relevant as human beings. In uncertain times, a strong will is more critical than a vital skill.

Human skills are Not Valued as They Should Be

From the moment we set foot in the world, we are naturally equipped with soft skills. We are gifted with imagination, creativity, emotions, empathy, and compassion. Currently, these skills aren't always valued in economic terms. If they were, Mother Theresa would have been a billionaire, but despite her considerable influence, she was never fiscally comparable to Jeff Bezos or Mark Zuckerberg.

Our children are taught to draw between the lines, sit on their chairs, stop dreaming, and keep their mouths closed. Skills like compassion, intuition, empathy, emotions, ethics, and curiosity are not the primary focus in schools. They should be.

Hard skills can be replaced. But a strong sense of purpose and powerful motivation cannot. They are uniquely human qualities that are going to become ever more valuable.

So How Do We Stay Ahead of the Machines?

Some experts estimate that the majority of the jobs in our current economy are based on hard skills. The harsh reality is that the human body is not well equipped to perform anything for long periods without significant strain. The most valuable skills that take people years to learn also involve us making a lot of expensive mistakes during the learning process. Skills aren't easily interchangeable either, making us somewhat inflexible.

Businesses will expect more and more routine tasks to be done by A.I. or by robots, and I'm expecting that to happen within a decade. In the internet wave, we witnessed media becoming a commodity. Spotify offers music for a fixed monthly fee, Netflix provides entertainment at a low cost, and platforms like X and Facebook offer real-time news. In the AI wave, we're witnessing the emergence of hard skills as a commodity.

The Many Layers of Human Intelligence

Although AI is developing at an astonishing pace, it's crucial to remember that human intelligence operates on levels far beyond the reach of any algorithm. We often mistake intelligence for the narrow cognitive layer, the part of our mind that reasons, analyses, memorises, and computes. But that's only a small fraction of what truly makes us human. In fact, only about ten to fifteen percent of our total capacity is cognitive, the portion that our education systems train, our companies measure, and our societies reward.

Beneath this thin cognitive crust lies a vast landscape of deeper intelligences that give life its texture, colour, and meaning. Around eighty-five to ninety percent of what we call human intelligence is not about logic or memory at all. It's emotional, intuitive, creative, social, and moral in nature, the invisible architecture of consciousness that shapes every thought, feeling, and action we take.

- Our emotional intelligence allows us to sense what another person feels without a word being spoken. It guides empathy, compassion, and self-awareness the subtle wisdom of the heart.
- Our social intelligence connects us to the collective. It enables us to cooperate, to lead, to build trust and belonging within families, communities, and organisations.
- Our creative and imaginative intelligence lets us see patterns where none seem to exist, to dream of futures not yet born, and to turn ideas into form.
- Our intuitive and somatic intelligence speaks through the body, through the gut sense that knows before the mind does, through the subtle awareness that detects coherence or danger before we can explain why.
- And our moral and existential intelligence gives us direction. It is the inner compass of values, integrity, and purpose that orients us toward meaning and truth.

Together, these layers form the true spectrum of human intelligence. They are interwoven like threads in a living tapestry, each one amplifying the others. And it's precisely this multidimensional intelligence that no machine can replicate.

AI can process data faster than any brain on Earth. It can store, sort, and predict patterns with breathtaking precision. But what it lacks is understanding. Knowledge without context is just noise. True understanding arises only when knowledge passes through the filters of experience, emotion, and embodied awareness. It's something that grows from living, through the senses, through intuition, through the endless loop of trying, failing, feeling, and learning again.

Machines can know everything about the world, but they cannot feel their place within it. They cannot taste joy or grief, cannot sense beauty, cannot stand in awe of life itself. And perhaps that's where our greatest evolutionary advantage lies, not in the speed of our thinking, but in the depth of our feeling. AI may master cognition, but humanity will always master meaning.

There is Good News for Team Human

For the first time in history, we share our planet with systems that appear to know almost everything. AI can recall more facts than any human being could in a thousand lifetimes. It can calculate, categorise, and connect information faster than our fastest thought. It can even simulate our language, mimic our tone, and generate insights that look almost human. But beneath that dazzling surface lies a fundamental gap, a void between knowing and understanding.

Knowledge Without Experience

AI is built on data. Every answer it gives is a reflection of something it has seen before. It recognises statistical patterns and rearranges them in new forms, but it has never felt a sunrise, smelled the ocean, or held a hand trembling with emotion. It knows about light but has never seen the dawn. It knows the chemistry of tears but has never cried them.

That's because real understanding cannot be downloaded; it must be lived. True understanding arises from sensory experience, how something feels, smells, tastes, moves, and resonates within us. It's the embodied intelligence that connects neurons to emotions and turns knowledge into meaning.

The Portuguese neuroscientist Antonio Damasio once wrote, "We are not thinking machines that feel; we are feeling machines that think." His research showed that emotion isn't the opposite of reason, it's the foundation of it. Without emotion, humans can't make meaningful decisions. Patients with damage to the parts of the brain responsible for emotion can still calculate logically, but they become paralysed when asked to choose. They can list every rational option, yet can't decide what's best. The missing ingredient is feeling, the quiet intelligence that gives thought its direction. AI has no such compass. It can rank options, but not value them. It can predict outcomes, but not care about them.

From Information to Meaning

Modern cognitive science has shown that understanding emerges from what's called embodied cognition. Researchers like Francisco Varela and Eleanor Rosch demonstrated that our minds are not isolated computers in our skulls, they are living systems shaped by the body's interaction with the world. We don't merely process information; we participate in it. Our understanding grows through movement, emotion, and context.

When a child learns what "hot" means, they don't study the concept, they touch, feel, withdraw, cry, and remember. The body learns before the intellect does. That moment of sensation carries emotional weight, and it transforms abstract data into understanding. AI can process billions of data points about temperature, but it will never flinch from the heat. It will never know what it means to be burned, and therefore, it will never understand "hot."

The Missing Spark

Understanding is not about storage; it's about transformation. Each experience we live reshapes the neural pathways in our brains. Every emotion, mistake, and insight re-wires the connections that make us who we are. That's why human intelligence grows deeper with age, with love, with loss, with life itself.

AI systems don't grow in this way. They scale, but they don't mature. They expand, but they don't evolve in consciousness. The scientist Iain McGilchrist, author of 'The Master and His Emissary', describes how the left hemisphere of the brain seeks control and certainty, while the right hemisphere seeks context and connection. True understanding, he says, emerges only when both work together. AI operates entirely in the left hemisphere, it knows the map, but not the territory.

Humans live inside the territory. We navigate through uncertainty, we interpret symbols, we sense intentions. Our understanding is fluid and alive, born from a dynamic conversation between heart, mind, and body.

The Hopeful Difference

This is our advantage, and our hope. While AI accumulates more and more knowledge, humans can cultivate deeper understanding. We can listen beneath the surface, feel patterns, sense coherence, and find meaning in chaos. As the cognitive layer of intelligence becomes automated, we are being invited to rediscover the rest of ourselves, to awaken the emotional, intuitive, and moral dimensions that make us whole. AI may help us remember what it means to be human.

Because understanding is not an algorithm; it's a relationship. It lives in the space between experience and awareness, between the heart and the world. It's what turns data into wisdom, and wisdom into compassion. So, I believe what can't be digitised or automated will only increase in value. As technology takes over more and more of our hard skills—the analytical, repetitive, and procedural work—our soft skills will rise in importance. Businesses will soon be financially motivated to cultivate qualities that once seemed intangible: empathy, creativity, communication, intuition, and moral judgement. These are the new frontiers of value creation.

In fact, research already shows that soft-skill–intensive occupations are growing 2.5 times faster than other jobs. The more technology optimises the cognitive layer, the more human value shifts toward the emotional and relational layer. The differentiator of the future won't be how fast we think, but how deeply we connect.

That's why education, leadership, and organisational design must evolve. We must stop training people only to know and start nurturing their ability to understand. We need workplaces where emotional intelligence, ethical reasoning, and imagination are not "nice to have," but essential. Because in a world where machines know everything, the most valuable people will be those who can still feel something real. AI will continue to know more. But we will continue to understand more deeply. And that depth—our capacity to feel, to imagine, to connect, is what will guide us through the age of artificial intelligence.

Chapter 39

Impact On Our Jobs and Skills

The 6th wave will lead to an invasion of smart autonomous devices and robotics that will profoundly impact how we do our jobs every day and create value. In the next five years in the 15 largest economies, millions of jobs will disappear or radically change.

Current rules and industrial process automation works very simply. They follow a decision tree with pathways of branching decisions based on specific pre-programmed criteria: if this happens, then do that. This is straight forward automation, but AI changes that because it learns on its own and adapts in real-time. It can make variations on certain routines to adapt better to the process. This will have a deeper impact than a lot of people realise. It will impact the majority of jobs. Consider truck drivers, forklift drivers, accountants, and people who work in banking and insurance. Many of these jobs can be automated, maybe not 100%, but 70%-80% will be.

Anything that we can define with rules, can, in principle be automated. The economic value that many of our current skills add, will be squeezed out and just fade away when we can automate the task and the decision making needed to get to the stated outcome.

So, if you do machine-like work that contains repetitive tasks, soon machines will be better, faster and cheaper than you. AI doesn't need holiday or a pension plan. They get a 24/7 worker with none of the headaches.

A Crisis of Identity

AI has shown the potential to replace many tasks, including those traditionally associated with high-status professions like doctors and lawyers. As AI technology advances, it's not only the jobs themselves that are at risk, but the personal identity and self-worth that go with them. Many of us derive a sense of pride, purpose, and social status from our jobs. Losing these roles to machines will create an identity crisis for those whose sense of self is tied to their profession.

For doctors and lawyers, the potential for AI to take over many of their tasks is already being felt. AI can analyse medical images, make diagnoses, and suggest treatment plans with a high degree of accuracy. It can help lawyers do document reviews and legal research. As machines can perform them with great efficiency and accuracy means some aspects of these professions will be automated.

As machines take over, people will need to find new ways to derive meaning and purpose from their lives. This may involve rethinking what it means to be a professional, or finding new areas of work that can't be easily automated. Society will need to shift its focus from valuing people solely based on their job status to valuing individuals instead for their unique skills and abilities. Millions of people will have to explore new areas of interest and skill development to adapt to the changing work landscape.

Organisational Advantage, From Hard Skills to Heart Skills

For organisations, the potential advantages are immense. Around 80% of our economy is based on repetitive tasks, so we will have to differentiate ourselves to stay ahead of the machines.

I believe we need to let machines do the work with chips, and we must do the work with our hearts.

There are always going to be tasks that can't be automated, and we would be well advised to start taking advantage of the non-automatable premium. Our emotions, integrity, and compassion are hard to automate and there'll be a scarcity of them in a robotised world. We need to start rediscovering them.

What Will Jobs Look Like in the Future?

The core of this new economy comes down to collaboration between people in creative, fluid teams. The skills needed to stay connected to others include emotional intelligence and empathy. Our creativity is already expressing itself in many new professions. On YouTube, people record their interests, learnings, experiences, opinions or hobbies and many get hundreds of thousands, even millions, of views. Many earn decent money from their creative expression. There's also a massive growth in online learning. People with specialist knowledge give lessons, courses, and masterclasses on all kinds of subjects. Many niches with numerous small subcategories have emerged where people can indulge their passion.

Even if you only have minimal expertise, you can make your contribution in a particular field via a swarm.

Abundant New Professions

High street shopping is dying and physical stores are hardly needed anymore. It's online stores that need building. E-commerce platforms and digital transaction mechanisms are what are needed today.

The Internet apps of today are created by people doing jobs that hadn't been imagined 20 years ago. Many new professions have emerged in recent years. Take game designers. What started as a tiny niche club, has grown into a sector utilising millions of people worldwide, collaborating internationally creating millions of games. There are digital artists using tablets to create beautiful works of art used in those games, advertising, logos, corporate identities, on websites and in apps. You don't need to go to art school anymore, you just need to be able to produce great work.

Artistic work and wide scale collaboration is going to become a larger share of the economy. More people are becoming producers of AI video content of film footage, from photos to music clips that anyone can buy. That would have only have been available to large corporates a few years ago.

You no longer have to commission or film everything yourself to make a film. For a fixed monthly fee, you can create, generate or buy film clips, photos or sound clips, making it easy to produce something really professional. In every subsection of the creative economy, there is a growth of new professions and skills, driven by our creative human side.

The future of work will herald many new roles, we will see AI ethicists, longevity coaches, and other surprising roles we don't know we even need yet. When machines have automated many of our deficiency needs, we will focus on our growth needs, and our work will reflect that.

Invest in Your Own Unique Value

To ensure your own value to the future economy you will need to get closer to yourself. Stay tech savvy. Find out what your passion is. Start thinking about how you could bring that into your everyday work and make the world a better place based on your own passion and purpose.

"The greatness of a humanity is not in being human, but in being humane."
Ghandi

We need to become more humane in our dealings, in our empathy, and in the compassion that we show to each other. When we can, we will start seeing a change in the world that's not going to come from technology, it's going to come from within us.

Chapter 40

Soft Skills In a World of Commodities

Big tech companies are looking for people with these soft, human skills. Critical thinking is one of those key skills. Critical thinking skills allow us to analyse information and make sound judgments, especially important in a climate where main stream media tells you what your leaders want you to hear.

Tune into some alternative media channels and you will soon have enough information to start thinking for yourself. Algorithms give us echo chambers, so to keep learning and be able to think critically you need to seek out alternative points of view - even ones you don't agree with. It's impossible to think critically when you only consider one side of an equation.

The Future Economy

Emotional intelligence and the ability to communicate effectively will be essential in the coming wave of holographic technology. We will be in touch with global team members in real-time in a way we aren't familiar with today. Making a human-to-human connection, and keeping it, becomes super important in a virtual environment. Continuous dialogue will be what's needed inside fluid organisations.

Staying connected when things are going well is easy, but there's great skill needed to keep that connection healthy in difficult times.

More organisations are becoming purpose-driven with their main goal going beyond pure profit alone. In voluntary organisations the sense of well-being in teams is very high, because people share a common values-based purpose. Many people in the younger generation value meaning more than status or bonuses. Owning an expensive car is not the status symbol it once was. That trend will continue.

Younger people who have grown up in a society where everything is on-demand, don't seem to have the same drive to own things. They only want to have access to a specific resource or service when they really need it. That's the future we're heading for.

Status Going Down -Meaning Going Up

As status becomes less important, meaningful work will become more important. Younger people show us this trend is getting more traction. They are asking why we do what we do, what it contributes and who will benefit. Focusing on your purpose will help you to future proof yourself.

Your purpose is not a final destination. It's more of an alignment with who you really are. Being flexible is invaluable as we move towards more fluid organisational structures, because you'll be working with people in different compositions all the time. There'll be different teams with different constellations and constant change.

After my keynotes, people often ask me, "Christian, what does that future look like? I don't see it. I get that we're moving in that direction, but I don't see how organisations would work together in a swarm. I don't see what future government looks like if that's not a top-down structure anymore."

We need to be curious about new technology, other organisational structures, and other government structures. If we're curious enough, we'll find out which models work - and which don't.

First, we have to imagine it, then design it, and then we can start building it.

There are many issues where there is no clear right or wrong, so we are going to have to come together in cohesion to find a solution which is workable for everyone. This can only be done when people act with integrity and a strong set of values. Our needs and our behaviours are a fairly stable factor in this whole thing. Ethics are going to come more to the fore. AI, holographic technology, nanotechnology, are all going to throw a whole raft of new issues at us.

Mirror Mirror On The Wall

Technology behaves like a mirror that reflects our inner world. The sentence sounds simple but the implications are far reaching.

Today, much of our identity comes from our external environment; possessions, money, status, our education, connections and relationships, skills, job or job title. We cling to them, but what happens when technology digitises them, virtualises them, and turns them into a commodity?

Well, as more and more layers of 'stuff' are taken away, eventually we will be left with the core of who we are. Our whole identity is going to have to be reimagined and rebuilt. If you think of yourself as an accountant, doctor, lawyer, notary or a pilot, it won't be long before large parts of these professions will be performed by AI. When your job has been automated, what are you left with?

Technology acts like a mirror, giving us a reflection of our inner world. The more powerful technology is, the brighter the mirror becomes and the better reflection we get of our inner world. The intentions that we put into technology, are reflected in our outside world.

We've talked about platforms like META (Facebook) that when developed with the wrong intentions, have negative effects on people. They cause us to react and realise we don't want them in our lives. That's feedback taking place. I call that process Humanification in my first book.

The mirror effect of technology constantly confronts us with our own behaviour. The faster and more powerful technology gets, the faster and shorter that feedback loop gets. It's a process of awareness we are going through right now.

We are constantly confronted with our own actions, and with our own output. The harder we go into that outside world with all kinds of technology and possibilities, the harder that feedback comes back at us.

That's the 'Go digital, Stay Human' story. We go digital fast, but in doing so, we encounter all kinds of issues that force us to ask ourselves: what do we actually want to do with it?

The mirror effect is there continuously. It's like the infinity symbol (sometimes called the lazy eight because it looks like a figure of 8 on its side). It's a visual representation of the mirror effect I'm trying to explain; an infinite feedback loop. The faster technology goes, the faster that eight turns and the faster we get feedback.

The loop has speeded up. Just fifty years ago, we were dumping plastic into the oceans. It took fifty years to figure out we have created a plastic soup that's in our fish, our food, and even in our bodies.

Thankfully, the new waves coming at us now are so powerful and the feedback is so fast, we won't have to wait fifty years because today's technologies give us instant feedback. If we do something wrong, it blows back in our faces with no time to react.

With AI and holographic technology, we'll get instant feedback. If what we send out isn't authentic and doesn't have the right intentions, we will have instant feedback. The learning and awareness process is continuously accelerated by technology, just like a mirror. It's true for individuals, organisations, and society as a whole. The change that we would like to see in the outside world starts in our inner world, where all change begins

'Do not try to fix whatever comes in your life, fix yourself in such a way that whatever comes, you'll be fine'.
Sadhguru

Technology is an amplifier, and the more powerful it becomes the more powerful the amplification. It becomes increasingly important that there is something positive inside ourselves to amplify and critical to have a strong sense of purpose, be intrinsically motivated, with a robust set of soft skills to connect with others. We can all have a meaningful impact on our world while living our purpose.

So, before you try and tinker with things in the outer world, try to upgrade your inner world first. When we upgrade ourselves at the software level, our output becomes much better.

Many people ask me what future humanity will look like. I believe our hardware (our body) is almost fully developed, but our software still has a long way to go. To collaborate as one big super-organism in harmony and peace requires a huge improvement to our software.

Chapter 41

Ethics And Responsibility

Each wave solves problems and creates new issues at a higher level. AI technology will impact our privacy and future freedoms.

Freedom is a uniquely human value. Personally, it's one of my most important ones. It's fundamental to our very existence. We all value the freedom to decide what to do, who to meet, and what information you choose to share with others.

One of the most significant challenges will be how we use technology ethically and responsibly. How do we deal with bad actors, whose intent is to harm us for personal or political gain?

In the first layer, we developed governments to keep negative elements of society in check and provide the infrastructure society needed. However, now those governments are attempting to control and dominate more and more areas of our lives. Governments are exercising increased levels of power, abusing technology to influence and contain people.

In the first stage of every technology s-curve, technology is often used from an ego perspective. This is when it is developed and operated from a standpoint of dominance, power and control, functioning from a deficiency needs mindset.

The first GPS sensors were used in cruise missiles. Today, GPS is in all kind of devices that make our lives better. Technology development is often led by the defence industry and used to dominate or secure resources. It's only later that it finds its way into the mainstream and gets used for more benign and useful things. Most of the technology in your smartphone originated in the defence industry; the touchscreen, GPS sensor, gyroscope, motion tracking sensors, the LCD screen, wireless data transmitters & receivers and many, many more.

The benefits are present in many of the products and services that we use every day.

All new technology brings with it certain responsibilities and risks. When it's used for social good and to make our world a better place, all is well. But when it gets into the wrong hands, it can have disastrous consequences. The battle has already begun.

We are reaching the point that a small group of people can control whole countries, regions and even the world with these technologies, if we aren't careful. There is a danger that overarching totalitarian systems could emerge that encompasses the whole of humanity. We are increasing moving towards a totalitarian technocratic system where everything and everyone can be controlled and monitored.

AI has led to an explosion in facial recognition, with high-resolution security cameras recognising people from hundreds of meters away. They can even identify people from their unique movement patterns. You can be followed by automated cameras without even knowing.

In some countries this is already widely used. In China 1.2 billion Chinese have almost 700 million security cameras using advanced recognition technology trained on their activities. In the West, we rebelled against that, yet London has one of the highest number of surveillance cameras per head of population anywhere outside China.

AI-powered surveillance systems are capable of intercepting communications, following people and objects around and tracking and tracing in real-time. This is an application of technology that we definitely don't want - and we should stand up against it when we start to see it happening. Countries like China may have preceded us, but we're seeing the same themes emerging in Europe. We must be highly vigilant.

Pressure has resulted in a policy shift for several major big tech companies, including IBM, Microsoft, and Google. They now say they are not going to make this kind of technology available for defence purposes, police, or law enforcement (at least that's their official position). However, we don't know what's being sold under the table. Public opinion has led to this becoming a taboo way make money.

Society can exert pressure and give direction to the use of technology. On a personal level people are happy to use security cameras for their own wellbeing. Doorbell and home surveillance cameras allow you to see who comes to your property and keep an eye your pets while you are out. Though even here concerns have been raised that China (where many of these goods are manufactured) could hack in to millions of homes if they wanted to. We have to lay down more ethical agreements in the programming code, and think very carefully about what goes into it.

Moral Dilemmas Await

Suppose you have an autonomous car. At some point, it's likely the car will get into an emergency situation and has to deviate. Does it crash into the old lady with a walking frame, or crash into the young woman with a stroller? Or does it drive into a wall and endanger the people inside the car? These kinds of choices are made in a split second somewhere in the world every day, but when we create algorithms to control cars we have to think about them in advance of that split second crisis.

Such ethical issues are always up for discussion. There's mainly a value driven consensus on what the right decision would be - on a theoretical level, at least. As soon as we start to have to state them explicitly in code to start programming devices like robots, drones and cars, things get more complex. Code is no longer a single programmers' issue, it becomes a wider societal issue. How should these kinds of devices behave in an emergency?

Many ethical issues we haven't really had to deal with until now are surfacing. They are already a challenge on social media. These platforms connect us, but they exert a level of control over us too. If you are sceptical, take a look at a documentary on Netflix called "The Social Dilemma". It makes you aware of how social media platforms work and that we, the people, are not the customer, we are the product..

You Are The Product

Social media companies have the power to control our personal information, manipulate our emotions, and shape the way we think.

Algorithms determine what we see, do, and even what we believe. They can have a profound impact on our mental and emotional well-being, as well as on our ability to make informed decisions.

The power wielded by these companies is their ability to shape public opinion by controlling the information we see. That can stifle dissent and limit our exposure to a diversity of ideas, opinions, and perspectives. The result is a homogenisation of thought and a lack of critical thinking with serious implications for the health of democratic societies.

Many Tech companies started with good intentions. Sergey Brin and Larry Page founded Google with the belief that privacy was the most important thing, and weren't going to bother people with ads. But as they grew bigger, the new CEO Eric Smith, brought in new investors with a different view. The priority for privacy was out and they started profiling people and offering relevant ads. Profits grew by 3,500%. Then they grew even faster so they needed more money. Big hedge funds came on board who invested with strings attached. Once cherished principles went overboard for big money. That's how new startups get polluted with an old mindset.

META (Facebook) started with good intentions. In the documentary 'The Social Dilemma' it becomes clear that people think they use social media. In reality, it's the other way around, social media uses us! The vast majority of social media platforms are data factories, milking users for detailed data profiles. They get as much data and metadata from you as possible to predict your behaviour. Every picture you post, every word you use, how you construct your sentences, the locations you visit, are all being tracked. That data says something about you, what kind of decisions you make and your behaviour. They can predict what kind of products you will buy, what car and holiday you want, and more. The better they do that, the more relevant ads they serve to you and the more profit they make. It's not about you at all. It's about your data profile, and you're valuable.

At META there's been one big data scandal after another. The Cambridge Analytica affair saw millions of data profiles sold to outside parties, who created political profiles to manipulate people towards certain voting behaviours. We can ask the companies to change, but it's in their DNA and regulation lags way behind their behaviour. Scandals have led to META being one of the top fifteen most hated companies. They still millions on the platform, but have trouble hiring. People don't want to work there anymore despite great pay. In terms of ethics and responsibility, they are making rather a mess of it and long term, it's will work against them. META and their competitors are all competing for the smartest programmers and algorithm experts. If they don't want to work for them, they have a problem.

META say at conferences that the future is private, but people don't trust them. They've shown over and over again that they don't care about people and their privacy. What they do care about is gathering and selling data for profit. More and more people are jumping to other platforms.

One of those platforms is MeWe, a kind of Facebook concept but one that respects privacy and wants to empower people by connecting them to others. When one company takes things too far, other platforms appear and offer alternatives.

When a great deal of power is held by a few individuals, it often goes wrong. Power corrupts, and absolute power corrupts absolutely. It's no different with tech companies. They can control and influence the social debate for their own gain, but they create wider social problems when their intentions are not aligned with the intentions of society. Companies want to maximise profit, but society wants more connection and to come up with solutions together.

Until we get tech companies aligned with our societal goals, these platforms are dangerous developments, because whoever controls the technology controls public and political debate. That, in turn, controls how the world is governed. The powerful still control the output, it's only the medium that's changed.

A New Kind of Internet

The problems of privacy and control reside at a deeper level and to solve them we need to transition to a different kind of Internet. The current Internet is application based, meaning that all your data is stored in big applications and databases (applications include Facebook, Google, LinkedIn, YouTube). Your search results, clicks, product purchases, comments, and pictures you post, are effectively owned by them, not by you.

As long this continues our privacy isn't guaranteed and there's little transparency. We need to move towards systems that are based on equality if we want to maintain any sort of control of the ownership of our own identity. Once again, swarm organisations are probably the solution.

Swarm are self-governing entities and I believe that an entity based, decentralised and autonomous Internet is coming. It will give us our freedom to choose again.

Those entities can be people, autonomous cars, smartwatches, phones, or even thermostats. Remember, anything that can be digitised can be an entity. Every entity can have a 3D address and the relationship between them determines how much information can flow between them. This would solve many privacy issues. If you have a relationship with a family member you would be happy to share more information with them than you would share with your electricity company. So, the closer the relationship, the more you share information with that entity. That would become a mirror of how things are in real life. That's how the Internet should be.

As trust builds with a new entity (whether a person, brand or company), you can start sharing more information. If trust falls away, you can withdraw it again, because the information only resides in one place - with you. It's you that gives people access to it or not.

Sound like a fantasy? It isn't. People in the Netherlands are building that type of network already. The organisation is called Focafet and I believe this is the future of the Internet. It solves almost all privacy problems we're battling against in one fell swoop. But for this kind of platform to take off, people have to recognise the need for it.

It's up to all of us to educate ourselves about how our data is being used. Currently, when you sign up for an app or a service you probably don't read the T&C's. They can run to hundreds of pages of legal speak, so few people bother, it's designed that way! You accept them so you can get on and use the service. Although understandable, it's giving big tech the ability to censor what we see and control the information. The more people realise that, the more they will recognise need for alternative kinds of platforms where privacy is better regulated.

The line between empowering people with technology, and enslaving them, is fragile. Some tech companies are already responding by moving towards a more ethical and moral use of data. They may be small steps, but they are steps in the right direction. Apple's Screen Time app monitors how many times a day you use your smart phone and which applications you use. It makes you more aware of your addiction, giving you choices about your behaviour and online usage. Apple has also started to differentiate itself by pointing to privacy as becoming one of it's priorities. They know customers are concerned and are responding. The new campaigns about the iPhone are about privacy. Information is processed on your local device and goes into the Cloud, so it can't be tracked, traced, stored or viewed by other parties. Apple says very clearly: with us, you buy the product, you are not the product.

It's up to each one of us to consciously choose products, services and platforms that make the world a better place and not just the ones that make a few people rich. That is going to become a Unique Selling Point for more tech companies. People have now started to care more about ethics and in the near future, more people will choose brands that stand for strong values.

'With great power comes great responsibility'
Winston Churchill (and Spider Man)

Every big wave that brings new power brings new risks, and with them come new responsibilities. We must all take an increasingly responsible attitude and look from a more ethical viewpoint. We can use facial recognition, but do we really want this in our society? What is the right balance between safety and surveillance? These issues will become more politically influential as technology becomes increasingly powerful.

Chapter 42

Government Vs The People

The technology of the 6th wave is very powerful. In countries with less democratic regimes are using 6th wave technologies for ever higher levels of dominance and control of their citizens and increase their competitiveness with other countries. It's a new kind of arms race.

AI is almost as powerful, or maybe more powerful, than the atomic bomb. The country that achieves AI dominance first will have a huge advantage over the rest of the world. Powerful countries understand that and that's why there is now a full-on commitment to developing AI. Sadly, in many cases it's a commitment coming from the wrong intentions.

The Upside

Despite this, in the longer term I'm very positive about technology. If it gets into the hands of the ecosystem of the wider population, and isn't concentrated in the hands of governments or powerful individuals, it can be used for betterment.

As long as technology is in the hands of ego-systems, it is used for domination and control. But as soon as it gets into the hands of ecosystems, the community, citizens and wider society, it can do beautiful things.

Evolution Does a U-Turn

There is turning point, where evolution makes a U-Turn when we shift from a society driven by competition and ego, to a one driven by collaboration and ecosystems. We are in the middle of that turning point right now. This will be an intense time where technology will be abused to serve the old mindset so as a population we need to speak out against such abuse of power.

My research suggests that in the long run, the network (the ecosystem) always triumphs over power hungry individuals (the ego-system). The network is always smarter, more resourceful, and more powerful than individuals; no matter how powerful, mighty and rich these individuals are - eventually they fall.

We're seeing the old powers trying to control the internet, censor content, and filter out things they don't want us to hear, in a vain attempt to curtail our freedom of speech. It's happening with full force all over the world and people are fighting back. Because of centralised censorship, we're seeing the emergence of new alternative platforms no longer based on centralised ownership.

The counter-movement towards decentralised autonomous platforms can give us a bottom-up revolution. One where we are connect with each other and stand up against people and organisations who are doing their best to use technology against us.

Abraham Lincoln, former president of the USA, said "You can fool all the people some of the time, and some of the people all the time, but you cannot fool all of the people all of the time."

We have to stay awake to ensure the powerful new technologies coming in the 6th and 7th waves are used for the right purposes. We have to do everything possible to see that technology is taken out of the ego-systems hands and put into the hands of the ecosystem as soon as possible. If we can do that, the time we will spend in the cocoon phase will be limited. If we can't, we will endure a very unpleasant time inside the cocoon, until we can move on to the next phase.

Chapter 43

The Antidote - Re-Align With Nature

Our lives have become distant from the natural world in so many ways. Many kids think that food just arrives in plastic packaging, they don't even realise that meat comes from animals or that vegetables grow in fields. Whole generations have become so distant from the natural world that they hardly realise it is the very thing that supports their existence. Yet nature created us and has given us the tools to develop our world.

We need to get closer to her again, and quickly.

Technology's evolution mirrors nature's waves and cycles, yet we have become increasingly misaligned with it. We started out in alignment, our survival depends on re-aligning with it.

Before technological wave of the agricultural revolution, we were at one with nature, we lived in it 24/7. We ate from nature, our medicines came from nature and we were in flow with our environment.

As we developed more technological systems, from agriculture to transport and heavy industry, had food year-round. We lost our dependency on the seasons. We can now generate light, energy, and heat all year round and have created a constant and unnatural environment.

The more and more systems we develop, the more alienated from nature we become.

The more things we do under pressure, the further from nature we get.

The majority of people are even disconnected from their own bodies and their spiritual selves. Many of us are more connected with our smartphones than we are with our own bodies! We spend all day with our smartphone with global information coming at us constantly, yet we don't listen to what our own body is telling us. We only notice our physicality when it goes wrong.

We are at the extreme end of that curve. Though the more aware of our misalignment we get, the greater the opportunity for us to U-turn back towards nature again. Our ego-systems will have to transform into ecosystems if we want to live healthy lives.

The New Art of Listening

We are becoming more disconnected from the people we love. Are you sometimes more immersed in your phone than you are with the people sitting with you in the same room?

Maybe it's hard to get your partner's or kids attention because they are more focused on their device than they are on you. Instead of just calling people and hearing their voice, we send them a WhatsApp message. We experience relationships and our environment through our digital devices. It's time to rebalance and reconnect in real life again and make a conscious effort to spend time outside the digital domain.

The whole western style industrial economy has disconnected us from Mother Earth. Our industrial systems just aren't sustainable. We are draining Earth of her resources. Our systems are polluting the air, oceans, and our food. We've reached a peak and we really can't go much further.

Various models suggest that around 2040 we will reach a point of no return if we keep going in the same direction. We will have completely used up what the earth can give us without irreversible damage. It's time to change.

High rise living in cities is a standard way of packing more people into small spaces. Cities have become concrete jungles, unnatural, unhealthy environments disconnected from nature. We have health problems caused by our unhealthy lifestyles and screen addictions. Our answer? More chemicals.

We no longer instinctively fall back on natural principles and medicines. We are being pushed to believe the only way to heal is using pharmaceuticals. The focus is on vaccines, instead of strengthening our immune system, taking vitamins, sleeping well, natural medication, exercise, and natural ways to regain our health. We must take a stand.

Separation is a Killer

During COVID, a whole generation was separated from others. Lockdown limited our children's social development and millions were separated from loved ones. That's deeply unnatural. Connecting with others is part of who we are as humans. Lockdowns inflicted immense emotional damage. Our immune systems and our general wellbeing suffered too.

Connecting with people constantly trains our immune system. We were forced, in many countries, to alienate ourselves even more from nature. We have become sterile beings separated from the source of our existence. We wear protective clothing. We use household products to kill bacteria - even healthy ones. Our houses are more sterile. The delicate balance of microbes and bacteria that have formed part of our environment for generations are being wiped out and we live in fear.

I am convinced that the COVID crisis marked a turning point. As we drifted further and further away from nature during the pandemic, with enforced unnatural rules and systems, we became more aware of its importance.

It's not all bad news. The 6th layer of the Maslow pyramid is about restoring balance with our aesthetic needs for beauty, order, and symmetry. Maslow wrote, "humans need to refresh themselves in the presence and beauty of nature while carefully absorbing and observing the surroundings to extract the beauty that the world has to offer. This need is a higher level need to relate in a beautiful way with the environment and leads to beautiful feelings of intimacy with nature and everything beautiful."

He describes our need to feel at one with nature again. If we are going to thrive in a more technologically driven world we have to go back. But how do we do that?

Future Forms Are Organic

In the 6th wave technology is allowing us to create things in-line with nature once again. AI and 3D printers help us to create naturally, and that's reflected in next-generation products.

In my keynotes, I show a picture of a prototype wheel, it's a Michelin tyre with no distinction between the tyre and the rim of the wheel. It was created and built using generative design and 3D printing, working more like nature does. Using a virtual simulated environment, it evolved from hundreds of thousands of variants. AI picked those that worked well in the virtual evolutionary process, then printed out the resulting design in 3D.

We can structure and form products more in the way nature would. Companies like Festo are making robots inspired by natural principles. Festo's robotic arms look similar in structure to an elephant trunk. There are drones that fly like butterflies and robots that walk like lizards. Designers and programmers are taking inspiration from nature, using principles that work in the natural world and packaging them into technology.

Next generation buildings will have more organic materials and designs influenced by nature. Bamboo has a higher tensile strength than steel, but is weaker under compression; AI can use that data to engineer buildings using natural materials in locations where they are abundant.

We are designing buildings that can generate and store energy, reducing the need energy to be brought in. We can print advanced structures that look and behave like butterfly wings that can regulate temperatures inside buildings.

Many buildings erected over past decades are concrete monstrosities. We poured concrete into a wooden container, let it harden, and we had a building. But if we can 3D print in more natural forms, we can design differently, utilising more natural and complex structures and shapes.

Biomimicry is a design philosophy that studies how nature solves functional problems. It encourages us to look to nature instead of making minor incremental improvements to old designs. For example, a designer might start by asking how could we streamline a car based on how a cheetah is streamlined. Or streamline a boat using fish as inspiration, or an aircraft based on a bird. Analysing shark skin under a microscope gave us faster swimsuits with less drag in the water. Waterproof breathable fabrics came from studying lotus leaves.

What else has nature got that's even more streamlined than what we have today? Much of today's highly effective materials technology has come from this field, with more to come.

How to Feel Human Again

We can all align with nature again. We must listen to and feel our bodies again. To listen to our passion, our purpose and our heart. What gives us meaning? What makes us happy? What makes others happy?

If you will do that as an individual, and start to work with others who do the same, a new kind of organisation emerges that is more aligned with nature. The products and services that come out of them will be more aligned with nature too.

If we want to change the world, we have to start with ourselves. Just taking a walk in nature helps you to reconnect with it. So does spending time away from the artificial stimuli of your screens.

John Friend, an American yoga teacher said "Align with nature ...Magic happens."

I experience this every day. The more I listen to my heart, the more I engage with my passion, my purpose, the more I'm in flow, the more peace I find, the more beautiful things I see, and the more interesting people I meet.

It's so simple, yet it really works. So instead of reading about nature on your smartphone, start spending time in it. Have more wonder for it, and find peace with yourself. Trust me, beautiful things happen.

Chapter 44

Elevate Yourself to The Next Level

With the advent of AI, the facades we have built based on our jobs and artificial identities will soon be exposed. We will need to rely on deeper, more intrinsic qualities to define our own self-worth. As we move towards a time where an individual's soul may become their unique selling point, it is important to consider what really makes a person valuable.

While the idea of a purpose crisis may sound daunting, it's an opportunity for personal growth and exploration. Without the constraints of relying on superficial factors to define our value, we may be able to find new and more fulfilling ways to reshape it and contribute. It will challenge us and fuel demand for purpose and meaning in our lives and I believe we will be faced with this challenge within five to ten years.

As technology gets faster and cheaper, the automation wave will accelerate.

The positive flip side is that technology is stacking more empowering ecosystems on top each other. As more online platforms emerge, they allow us to monetise our creative expression and create new economic value.

We are moving from the bottom of the Maslow pyramid, where it's mostly about hardware, towards the top of the pyramid, where it is mostly about software.

The base of the pyramid is about hard skills, and organisations within it provide hardware. At the top it's mostly about soft skills, and the organisations within that are mostly software companies: Facebook, Google, YouTube, and X. They represent the skills humans were born with.

Technology platforms will increasingly boost our inner world. Just one person can have a huge positive impact and existing technology means you can reach millions of people. So, what are you going to inspire all those people?

It's becoming increasingly important that we all start asking ourselves, "if technology is an amplifier? What do I have in my inner world that's worth amplifying?"

During my education, and probably yours as well, there was no attention paid to purpose and meaning. You were guided towards a certain profession at a young age and given relevant subjects so you could advance towards specific skills and abilities. Then you started working and generated a certain economic value. Your purpose was to make money!

I believe that purpose in itself is also evolutionary. If you look at the first wave, the Agricultural Wave, the purpose was mainly to survive, to grow food. In the 2nd wave, the Industrial Wave, people built infrastructure and created a secure reliable environment. It's clear that each wave demands a different type of purpose from the people and organisations within it.

Within one working life, we are going to move through several waves, for which completely different purposes are needed. This will no longer just be measured by money, but by your social value.

Go East For Answers

Just as humanity must re-align itself with the natural ecosystems that sustain life, each of us must also re-align with our inner ecosystem, the subtle rhythms of purpose, curiosity, and joy that guide us from within. The principles that govern forests, oceans, and swarms also govern our inner world: balance, flow, and renewal. When we lose touch with these inner patterns, we experience the same imbalance that nature now reflects back to us.

Realigning with nature, therefore, is not just about restoring the planet, it is about remembering our place within it. The next step of evolution begins inside, as we rediscover the purpose that connects our personal life to the greater web of life itself. In Japan purpose has been embedded inside their culture for a very long time. The Japanese have a principle called Ikigai that's used in education and in many organisations. It's part of the DNA of Japanese culture.

Ikigai is this; your reason for being, for your existence. You can see in the constituent parts of Ikigai below. Where the four circles of your subjects overlap, you find your reason for being. Your Ikigai.

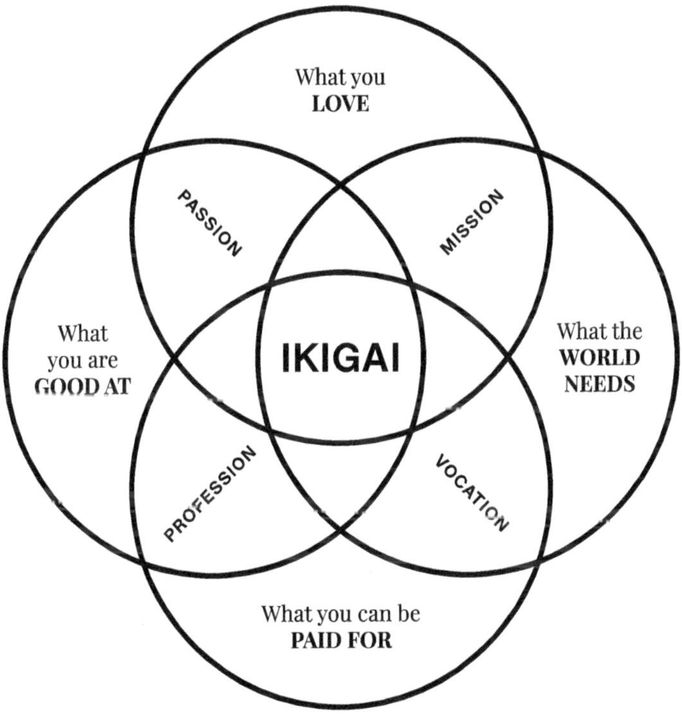

Finding Your Ikigai

There is a simple five-step process to discover your Ikigai. The first is to ask yourself questions.

The left petal asks - what are you good at, what are your talents?

The top petal asks - what do you like to do, what do you love, what do you really enjoy?

The right petal asks - what is valuable to your environment, what does the world need from you?

The bottom petal asks - what can you get paid for, what value can you add (societal or a monetary)?

To get started, write your first thoughts to these key questions. At the beginning of the process, there will probably be a lot of things in each petal. Simplify your answers by choosing the three things that appeal to you most.

Now, take a good look at the three topics you've prioritised. What do you feel when you visualise them? Did you write them down because they're authentic, or because you've felt you should? Maybe your education, expectations of others, or habitual ways of thinking influenced you. Did your answers come from deep inside you without judgement?

When your priority list of 3 feels right, go and test your ideas! Talk to people who know you well about your findings; colleagues, friends, and family.

Finally, when it feels good (and keeps feeling good), create an environment that supports you to develop your Ikigai. If you work five days a week, what if you could start working three or four using spare days to work on your Ikigai. If it's not possible, could you work on it at weekends? What could happen if you invested more time in your Ikigai journey?

Many of us will need to explore new and unconventional career paths that express our unique skills and talents. Exploring new areas of interest will mean taking risks, and finding ways to create value in non-traditional ways. By focusing on your Ikigai, you could find new and meaningful ways to contribute and define your worth. Your Ikigai is a very good place to start.

Chapter 45

Finding Your Flow

Psychologists split motivation into two key types, extrinsic and intrinsic. If you are working just for the pay-check because you have bills to pay, and you have to do work you hate, that's extrinsic motivation. When you do something because it really matters to you, not because you have to do, that's intrinsic motivation. Robotics and automation will take away so many jobs that there will be many people struggling to find meaningful work.

You are most likely to be intrinsically motivated when you do things that give you self-esteem, confidence, a sense of achievement, and that fulfil your need to be unique. These feelings sit at the top of the Maslow pyramid and once you are doing activities that sit in the top two layers you are making the most of your inner potential and in tune with your true purpose.

David Hawkins, the author of "Power versus Force", plotted levels of consciousness against emotions using a scale of 1-1000. He noted that when your conscious level is at the low of zero, you experience emotions like as fear and shame. At a level of a thousand, you experience emotions such as love, joy, and gratitude.

When you discover and work towards your Ikigai, you raise your level of consciousness. When you do things that make the most of your talents, you are in a positive emotional high consciousness state. You are spending time in flow. That's a measurable peak state of optimum consciousness where you feel and perform at your very best.

Being in flow has a profound effect on both your senses and physical performance. You've probably experienced flow yourself, or heard it talked about. It's is often described as an adrenaline rush, a eureka moment, or being "in the zone". In flow, your internal dialogue quietens, self-judgement stops and you get an incredible feeling of connection to where you are, and what you are doing. You have a laser focus and your creativity races off the charts. You can solve problems, explore novel solutions and increase your performance. Physically, your frontal lobe almost shuts down and overthinking and self judgement stops. Your brain wave frequency changes too, and performance enhancing chemicals flood in. You literally get out of your own way.

Thankfully, neuroscientists have decoded what triggers a flow state, so it's possible for you to reproduce it and exponentially improve your creativity and personal performance.

Flow is a very human characteristic, one that robots are unlikely to ever have. Finding flow is one of the key elements of a fulfilling, future proof life. It will help you do great work you feel good about, and help you find deeper satisfaction in your personal life.

I believe that flow plays a huge part in the future of high-performance humanity. Learning about it and being able to tap into it will help you design a future in which you can navigate the technological changes ahead.

Negative emotions block flow. Shame, guilt or anger keep people stuck in a level of consciousness, locking them in a cycle of inertia where they are motionless unless pushed to act; or are hyperactive and force things to happen. Either route pushes us to burn out. Negative states make it hard to move towards anything positive.

When positive emotions dominate people become pro-active. Trust, courage, and optimism help people raise their consciousness levels. They become happier and more productive. People perform at their best without stress, and in flow extraordinary outcomes happen. Joy, gratitude and love dominate. The more aligned with your passion and purpose you get, the more you experience flow.

McKinsey and Co. did a ten-year study of CEO's and business leaders of large organisations and discovered that when leaders are in a flow state, they are 300-500% more productive than they are in their 'normal' state. What emotions do you experience the most in your daily work? Which state are you most often?

Like most things, flow exists on a curve. At the end of the curve people are disengaged, not interested, happy or productive. At highest end people are overwhelmed; things are too much. Flow is found in the middle. You need just the right amount of information and just the right amount of time. Then people are extremely productive and efficient.

Mihaiy Csikszentmihalyi, grandfather of flow who spent his life studying it, identified its key ingredients. They are:

- Complete concentration in the moment
- Immediate feedback
- Clear goals
- Just the right level a level of challenge

The final point he called The Challenge-Skills Ratio; too low a challenge you lose interest. Too high and you get overwhelmed then quit. Designers of computer games know this. They design games that put players in a flow state. If they are too difficult you back out of the game, too easy and you find something else to do.

With crystal clear goals it's easier to motivate yourself to take action in a specific direction. When you're confident a goal is viable, you start your journey very differently.

It's usually obvious if your activity moves you closer or further away from your goal and that helps with feedback. Your goals must be your own and your direction a personal choice. With freedom of choice, you choose the path that works for you.

Physical activity is often a flow trigger too. Athletes spend more time in the zone, and know how to access it, than most people do. That's because movement releases powerful chemicals, and when you do something physical requiring focus, your brain is too busy coordinating your body to think of ways to inhibit your performance.

You don't even need to do high levels of activity for flow chemicals to start flooding your brain. Any co-ordinated movement helps get the judgemental part of your brain out of the way. Just a brisk walk changes your brain chemistry. Activity that challenges your coordination helps, whether it's Tai-Chi, drawing, or gardening, they all challenge your brain with to deliver precision coordination. Given the right combination of stimuli, flow gives you a feeling of total immersion and centred-ness.

In flow, your perception of time changes. Neuroscientists call this "time distortion". Have you ever been so focused doing something you thought a few minutes had past, then realised an hour had gone by? That's time distortion. Even driving a car on a familiar route can result in your losing a sense of time. While your brain is engaged in the act of navigating and managing the car, your mind is partially elsewhere. You have probably experienced a car journey when you get home at in what seems like no time at all.

There are short cuts to getting into flow. When you walk in nature or meditate your brainwave pattern changes. In that more relaxed state, alpha brain waves are triggered. That's part of the flow experience.

If you have ever had a great idea while walking the dog, having a shower, or driving, now you know why.

Getting into flow more frequently is a process of personal development. We can all give ourselves a helping hand to be get there more often. The first ten minutes of your day can set you in the right direction. While you are in the shower or exercising you are potentially triggering flow practice because, paradoxically, you're not in a high focus place. Your brain state is more likely to be in an alpha state naturally, making it easier to feel what's really going on in that moment.

If you want to go faster, you actually have to slow down first. You need to switch back and return to an alpha state. Then you get clear insight of what you have to do that day and listen to your feelings about how best to do it. The more you learn to listen to yourself, the more you find flow and the more aligned you get with your purpose or passion. It's a virtuous circle, but it doesn't happen completely on its own. You need to practice. Listen to your body and ask yourself; what do I feel like today? What comes easiest to me today?

It can help to go back in time in your mind. When you were a kid, what did you most love doing? If you were to create a timeline from your birth until today, when did you most experience joy? When did things flow easily?

When you start connecting to those moments, ask yourself if there's a common thread that connects them all. What were you doing? Why did things come so naturally?

We've been conditioned over the years to think a certain way. If you can, go back to the way of thinking you had before all your grownup complexities got in the way. Connecting your flow moment memories together is often the key that leads you to rediscover your purpose and your passion.

The late Steve Jobs, founder of Apple said not long before his death, "Stay hungry, stay foolish" and "The only way to do great work is to love what you do. If you haven't found it yet, keep looking. Don't settle".

So, keep looking. Search for your passion. When you are aligned with it, you will know. Flow is where the journey inward begins. It is the alignment of action, the point where doing and being, become one continuous motion. In flow, we remember what it feels like to move through life without resistance, guided by intuition rather than control. Once we taste that effortless harmony, the next step is inevitable: the awakening of awareness itself.

Chapter 46

A Spiritual Revolution - Driven By AI

Flow is more than peak performance; it is a momentary glimpse of unity, a preview of the spiritual revolution already unfolding. Flow is the bridge between science and spirit. In those moments when time disappears and action becomes effortless, something larger begins to move through us; a quiet intelligence beyond the thinking mind. The more we learn to surrender to this state, the more we begin to sense that flow is not merely a psychological phenomenon, but a spiritual one.

It reveals that consciousness itself is alive, dynamic, and interconnected, and that the same creative force driving evolution through technology is now awakening within us. This is the beginning of a spiritual revolution, one quietly accelerated by AI. As AI technology advances our social interactions, our personal development will be impacted too. We've talked already about finding purpose. I believe it goes even beyond that. I foresee a coming spiritual revolution where people turn more inward to explore their values, beliefs and sense of purpose in life.

We all reach a point when we confront our own mortality and sense the fleeting nature of the superficial elements of our lives. I'm convinced that people will seek to deepen their understanding of themselves and their place in the world.

The seeds have already been sown. There's already a huge expansion of the exploration of spiritual practices beyond traditional religion. Meditation, yoga, and mindfulness exploded and retreats become more popular every week. It's not surprising when you consider that so many of us have more connection with our phones, than we do with our friends.

Another symptom is the increase in digital nomad workers moving around the world to seek out satisfying work and a better quality of life. Growing numbers of digital nomad bases have been set up in low-cost locations with good weather, where people building digital products find like-minded collaborators, often ending up working together on joint venture projects. Governments are recognising this with many countries offering digital nomad visas. This trend has the potential to become very powerful in the face of the complex challenges facing society today, from climate change to social inequality, and it's set for massive further expansion.

As people become more spiritually aware and connected, it will hopefully lead to a greater sense of community and a willingness to collaborate towards common goals. The coming spiritual revolution is a natural response to the disruption of AI and a world increasingly domination by machines.

The AI wave is not just a technological revolution, it's an evolutionary invitation. The more intelligent our machines become, the more they illuminate what truly matters: not what we can do, but who we are.

Chapter 47

Your Future In a Nutshell

The developments dictating our future are converging, bringing a tsunami of unstoppable change that will take most people by surprise. But not you, you are more ready than most. We are being faced with an accelerated search for meaning.

Let's recap our key learnings.

Evolution and technology are both subject to the same forces of 7 waves, and we are at a tipping point today. AI is already at the point where the continuous doubling (or even quadrupling) effect of exponential growth means most people are massively underestimating how quickly the next wave is going to engulf us.

AI, holographic technology and the power of the swarm are going to radically change the world within ten years. Your daily life is likely to be unrecognisable to the life you live today. Technology has the power to free you from the drudgery of repetitive tasks and you will have time to discover who you really are, and what matters to you most.

Humanity's current predicament is one of dwindling reserves of non-renewable resources. Our governments and institutions are fighting for more control of both resources and citizens. We are all feeling the semi-controlled chaos and the tension that's generating as institutions are sensing their loss of power.

Their ego systems are under threat. The heavy handedness blocking our freedom of speech is evidence that instead of embracing the future, our governments are trying to wrestle control from citizens. They don't understand that nature is more powerful. The future of large government with no pushback from the population is over. They just haven't realised it yet.

We are in a difficult transition period. People want more freedom, not less. Citizen based technology is a genie that can't be put back in the bottle. That's good news for those of us who want the freedom to choose.

It's up to all of us to make our voices heard and participate in a more collective future that we can all influence.

Freedom of speech and freedom to choose are the cornerstones of individual identity. Those who want to minimise it are going to lose.

The mirror effect of technology gives us hope that things will get better. As we each expand our personal horizons, we have the personal power to make positive changes. We just need to tap into our inner freedom. Maslow showed us how it's natural to raise our levels of consciousness and overcome the dinosaur thinking our institutions cling to. We can be part of something better.

We have the foundations of a new kind of internet where we own our own data and can take back power from bad actors. We must pay attention and embrace the opportunity.

Many organisations will struggle through the transition. Some will survive, and some won't. You can't stop the evolution of technology any more than you can stop nature. It's going to happen, so we might as well get off the beach and surf the wave instead.

As we approach the spiritual revolution and step towards humanity 4.0, instead of being scared of AI, learn about it and embrace it. Equip yourself with more knowledge than your peers and be one of the few ready for what's coming.

Go through the Ikigai process. Find your passion and run with it. Detach from your devices from time to time. Make a conscious effort to go digital but stay human.

Don't allow yourself to be sucked into someone else's digital realm and lose valuable time that you'll never get back. Build more fulfilling relationships with your loved ones. Set a great example to those who look up to you.

Your inner self will be your most valuable asset, something that no robot or computer can ever take away. Nurture that, and nature will nurture you. Spend time in nature and explore what puts you into an alpha state. Connect with your body as well as your mind. You don't need to be busy all the time, it is during your moments of quiet reflection and connection with yourself (without distractions), that the genius inside you can reveal itself and grow into something magical.

Those working hard avoiding what's coming next will be blindsided. Remember that most people don't understand the forces of exponential change.

Those who make time to explore their inner selves will be able to embrace the future and thrive. You have the power to be one of them. You have the power to change. You have the power to be part of a wider shift in our consciousness and solve some of the world's greatest challenges.

Just like the flock of birds, you only need to connect to 6 or 7 others around you with a positive intention to become part of something powerful that, until now, we have only been able to dream about. Be forward thinking, embrace shifts in perspective and keep broadening your horizons. You have the power to change the world; one human being at a time. Start with yourself, find your spark, ignite your fire, and inspire others to do the same.

From the Head to the Heart

For centuries, the human mind has been our greatest source of progress.

It built bridges and cities, composed symphonies, decoded the genome, and reached for the stars. Thought became our superpower, our logic our compass, and knowledge our fuel. But now, as artificial intelligence begins to master the same cognitive abilities that once set us apart, we find ourselves at an inflection point. The more we outsource thinking to machines, the more we are invited to rediscover another, often forgotten, dimension of intelligence; the wisdom of the heart.

The Intelligence Beneath Thinking

AI can analyse faster, calculate more precisely, and remember infinitely more than any human mind. Yet for all its power, it lacks the one thing that gives intelligence its meaning: awareness. Awareness is not built on logic, it is born of presence. It emerges when perception meets feeling, when knowledge is infused with care, when data becomes understanding.

The heart is not the opposite of the mind; it is the completion of it. Where the mind seeks to understand, the heart seeks to connect. Where the mind dissects, the heart unites. Where the mind collects information, the heart transforms it into wisdom. As technology perfects the art of computation, it quietly releases us from it. In doing so, it guides us to the deeper intelligence that has always lived within us, one that feels, intuits, and resonates with life itself.

A Shift in Centre

We are shifting from a civilisation led by analysis to one guided by awareness. For millennia, our focus has been outward, on progress, production, and performance. But now, the direction of growth is inward. This inner shift is not regression; it is evolution. We are not abandoning reason; we are expanding it. We are not rejecting intelligence; we are rooting it in consciousness. The head and the heart were never meant to compete. They are two instruments of the same symphony, one tuned to logic, the other to meaning. When they play in harmony, a new form of intelligence emerges: coherent intelligence, a synthesis of thinking, feeling, and being. That coherence is the birthplace of creativity, intuition, and genuine innovation qualities machines can simulate, but never generate.

From Control to Connection

The story of the modern world has been one of control, mastering nature, optimising systems, and perfecting efficiency. But true evolution doesn't come from control; it comes from connection. We are rediscovering that what makes us human is not our ability to dominate complexity, but our ability to dance with it. To sense, adapt, and flow, like nature itself. The intelligence of the heart moves with this rhythm. It listens before acting. It feels before deciding. It leads without forcing. And it is this intelligence that will define the next era, not through equations or algorithms, but through empathy, intuition, and relational awareness. This is where the next revolution begins, not in silicon, but in synchronicity.

The Bridge to the Soul

When the mind and heart come into balance, something extraordinary awakens. A third layer of intelligence begins to shine through, one that doesn't just think or feel, but creates. This is the intelligence of the soul, the spark of consciousness that animates us from within. It is the quiet knowing that whispers beneath thought, the creative pulse that wants to express itself through your work, your relationships, your life. The journey from head to heart is not the destination. It is the gateway. It opens the door to something even deeper, to discovering and expressing your spark. Because once you reconnect with the intelligence of the heart, the question naturally arises:

- How do I live from this place?
- How do I bring soul into what I do?

That is the next step in our evolution, and the subject of the final chapter of this book: Finding Your Spark.

Chapter 48

Finding Your Spark

Putting Soul Into What You Do

We have reached a turning point. After all the waves of innovation, all the transformations and technological disruptions, we return to the most essential question of all: what makes us human?

We can now build machines that think, design, learn, and even create. Algorithms can compose music, generate stories, and paint pictures that move us. But there is one thing they can never truly replicate, the spark that lives inside us.

That spark is not knowledge, nor skill, nor logic. It is the invisible current that gives meaning to everything we do. It is the warmth behind your words, the intention behind your actions, the presence you bring into a moment. When you act from that place, you are not just performing a task, you are transmitting life itself.

AI can simulate intelligence. It can process emotion. It can mirror behaviour. But it cannot feel the impulse that gives rise to creation. It cannot sense the awe of beauty, or the joy of connection, or the quiet power of purpose. Those come from a deeper source, the human soul.

We are not simply intelligent; we are aware that we are intelligent. We can reflect upon our thoughts, question our motives, and give meaning to our experiences. This reflexive consciousness, this ability to observe ourselves in the act of living, is the essence of what it means to be human.

That is something no machine can do. AI can process data about experience, but it cannot experience itself. It can model emotions, but it cannot feel them. It can simulate choice, but it cannot choose with intention or moral weight. It can imitate empathy, but it cannot truly care. Our uniqueness lies not in our processing power, but in our capacity for presence, to be fully aware, connected, and alive in the moment.

From Human Doings to Human Beings

For more than a century, we have defined ourselves by what we do. Our value was measured in output, efficiency, and performance. We became "human doings," busy, productive, and exhausted. But now, as machines take over the doing, we are invited, or even forced, to rediscover the art of being.

Being is not passive. It is deeply active, but in a different way. It is the state of awareness in which creativity, intuition, and compassion arise naturally. From being comes clarity, inspired doing and action that is aligned with purpose, rather than driven by pressure. The next stage of evolution is not about having more intelligence, but about cultivating more consciousness. We don't need faster processors; we need deeper presence. We don't need bigger data; we need broader awareness. This is what the Fourth Industrial Revolution is really calling us to, a Fifth Human Revolution. One that moves us from efficiency to essence, from speed to stillness, from intellect to insight.

The Human Element

As technology grows more capable, the difference between what we do and why we do it becomes more important. In the coming years, almost everything that can be standardised, automated, or optimised will be. But soul cannot be automated. Presence cannot be programmed. If we fill our lives and organisations with routine, imitation, and noise, machines will not only match us, they will certainly surpass us. But if we bring curiosity, empathy, imagination, and genuine care into what we do, we move into a domain that no algorithm can enter. That is where your true value lies. That is where the human advantage begins. The most advanced form of intelligence is not artificial, it is authentic. It arises from coherence between head and heart, thought and feeling, logic and love.

The Soul Economy

The next economy will not be measured in productivity, but in authenticity. We are moving from the era of hard skills to heart skills, from producing more to creating meaning. People, organisations, and communities that operate from soul will thrive; those that don't will be automated, and fade into irrelevance. In this new Soul Economy, value arises from connection, not competition. From purpose, not performance. From coherence, not control.

AI will take the robot out of us. It's up to us to put the human back in. Our work will no longer be about efficiency alone. It will be about expression, expressing the unique frequency of who we are. Every act, every creation, every relationship will become a canvas through which our inner world shapes the outer one. The future of business, leadership, and creativity belongs to those who dare to lead with presence. To those who remember that energy, not information, is the true currency of human exchange.

Your Spark is Your Compass

Your spark is your inner navigation system. It is the signal that tells you when you are in alignment, when what you do, think, and feel are one. It's the sense of flow when time disappears, when effort feels like play, when you are fully alive.

Following that spark is not self-indulgence; it is about being in the service of your environment and being synchronised with it. Because when you do what lights you up, you light up others too. Your energy becomes contagious. It ripples through teams, families, and communities. It changes the field around you.

Machines can replicate output, but they cannot replicate aliveness. That is why your spark matters, not only for you, but for the whole system. It is how humanity evolves. Each time you act from your spark, you reinforce a new kind of intelligence, one that is integrated, embodied, and conscious. You become part of a living network that learns not through data, but through resonance.

The Future Resides Inside You

We began this journey by exploring how technology is reshaping our outer world. But the real transformation is happening inside us. As AI grows in intelligence, we are invited to grow in presence, and deepen our consciousness. The more advanced our machines become, the more essential it is that we act from awareness, compassion, and soul. That is our evolutionary task: to integrate head and heart, intelligence and intuition, logic and love. To remember that progress without presence is just acceleration, motion without meaning.

When you find your spark and put it into everything you do, you don't just stay ahead of the machines, you transcend them. You turn technology into an amplifier of your humanity instead of a replacement for it.

In the End

The future will belong to those who live and work with soul. Because soul is the one resource that never depletes, never becomes obsolete, and never needs an upgrade.

So, ask yourself:

- What lights you up from within?
- Where does your presence make a difference?
- What would the world lose if you stopped showing up as you?

The answers to those questions are your spark. Protect it. Nurture it. Share it.

Because in the end, our legacy will not be the intelligence we created, but the consciousness we awakened.

www.ingramcontent.com/pod-product-compliance
Lightning Source LLC
LaVergne TN
LVHW011512200926
848484LV00001B/16